T0117070

America:
A Country of Great Expectations

Sachin Anand Balram

iUniverse, Inc.
Bloomington

America: A Country of Great Expectations

iUniverse books may be ordered through booksellers or by contacting:

iUniverse
1663 Liberty Drive
Bloomington, IN 47403
www.iuniverse.com
1-800-Authors (1-800-288-4677)

ISBN: 978-1-4502-8446-2 (sc)
ISBN: 978-1-4502-8444-8 (ebook)
ISBN: 978-1-4502-8445-5 (dj)

Library of Congress Control Number: 2011900021

Printed in the United States of America

iUniverse rev. date: 2/10/2011

To those millions of immigrants who came to the United States of America to achieve the American Dream of prosperity, happiness, and success by working hard and by making huge sacrifices.

Contents

PREFACE

During my three decades in this wonderful country, I have come across hundreds of immigrants from different countries who are still not quite sure what their rights are, where they should turn in times of desperate need, and how numerous major systems and agencies function. How can they get the benefits from their taxes? How can they reassert their rights with authorities? Some of them have been in this country for several years and still do not know how the health-care system operates and what to do if they do not have health insurance and become seriously ill. Some still do not know where to turn if the hospital sends them a hundred-thousand-dollar bill for a week's stay. Some of them still do not know the difference between the Medi-Cal and Medicare systems—and the list goes on. This sort of ignorance, apathy, and lack of information and knowledge on the part of my fellow immigrants made me wonder how I could provide—in a simple way—the big picture of agencies, authorities, culture, traditions, etc., that any newcomer to this country can read and educate himself. This book can be read and analyzed before the immigrant departs his homeland, or it can be read during his leisure hours when he arrives in the United States or while he is in transit here. It can also be kept by the bedside as a self-help book. I hope that this book will educate the newcomer to become familiar with the way things are done in the United States and about the numerous agencies and their functions. I have tried to give my perspective of this country. I have mentioned the good things and the bad things. I have tried to point out the important things that will touch an immigrant's life within the first three months in America.

I have tried to provide the big picture about things that are important to all Americans in making their lives easier since knowledge is power. This vision of providing the big picture to fellow immigrants is what has inspired me to write. The book can also be a good source of reference for the Native Americans as well.

Many US born native Americans have limited knowledge of their country and how its socioeconomic systems operate. I also try to depict the numerous challenges, trials, and tribulations that a new immigrant must face in order to establish himself in this country. I also provide some guidelines where help can be found and how it can be obtained.

I have attempted to provide some useful information relating to different systems, such as legal, health, and education, and have infused my own opinions about my adopted country. I have provided a few glimpses of my own experiences, discussing at length what I like about this country, what I dislike, what I miss about my old country, and how I have contributed to this wonderful country. I have tried to inject some humor in a few places and have provided some solid facts and figures along with useful hints, tips, and ideas for how to be cautious. This is so that the newcomer may avoid some hassles later on, such as how to rent an apartment and how to buy a used car. The quotations from prominent people I have used are pertinent and have a message to relay.

My intention is to reassure my fellow immigrants that they have chosen the best country in the world. There should be no second thoughts about migrating to America. At first, there may be lot of frustrations, struggles, and disappointments. There will be growing pains. However, with the passage of time, things will improve—provided one is willing to work hard and make many sacrifices. Millions of immigrants have come to this country and have managed to become wealthy and prosperous—and so can you. They live happily and have become model citizens. However, one must first get some basic facts and learn quickly as to how this country operates and how its democratic systems function.

The starting point of any new adventure should be to get the big picture and then plan how the adventure or the mission is going to be accomplished. I hope that this book will provide a starting point for the adventure.

I sincerely hope that, after reading this book, the reader will have more knowledge and a basic understanding of the different systems, agencies, ideologies, traditions, and customs that make the United States the greatest country on this planet. If one person can benefit from reading this book, I will consider my mission accomplished.

CHAPTER 1:
DESTINATION: SFO

"My conception of America is a land where men and women may walk in ordered freedom in the independent conduct of their occupations. A place where they may enjoy the advantages of wealth, not concentrated in the hands of the few but spread through the lives of all, where they build and safeguard their homes and give their children the fullest advantages and opportunities of American life. A land where every man shall be respected in the faith that his conscience and his heart direct him to follow, where content and happy people, secure in their liberties, free from poverty and fear, shall have the leisure and impulse to seek a fuller life."

—Herbert Hoover, October 22, 1928

We arrived at Nadi International Airport, Fiji, on a hot, humid Tuesday afternoon on December 19, 1979. My wife, Kamini, and our ten-month-old daughter, Suhani, and I had three pieces of luggage. I had FJ$500 in cash in my pocket. Luckily, at that time, one United States dollar was on par with one Fijian dollar. I wore a safari suit, and Kamini was gorgeously draped in a white and blue sari. The suitcases with our personal possessions were all that we owned. A few friends and family members had gathered

1

at the airport to bid us farewell. They all had the same question. "Why do you want to leave your country and legal profession when you were doing so well both personally and professionally?" Some joked that I had watched too many Hollywood movies and wanted to live life in the fast lane and predicted that this ambition would be my road to ruin. Some called me a "capitalist pig" and others seriously advised me that I had made a wrong decision and said that they would see me return in six months. A few others joked that, in America, all wives had two boyfriends on the side. Some opined that all American husbands were playboys. I listened, but did not know how to respond since I had never visited America. I had a very faint idea about what to expect. I knew that America was a country built by the immigrants. Millions went there, worked hard, and had lots of success. And, so could I.

I answered them diplomatically. "I just want to be closer to my parents and siblings and want to become a full-fledged attorney in California." I did not tell them—and most of them did not know that I would have to study California law and pass the California bar exams in order to practice in that state. I knew in my inner being that I could and would pass the bar. I had read about it and knew that it would be another tough exam that I would have to study for.

The next thing I knew, the Pan American flight took off over the South Pacific Ocean bound for San Francisco. As it lifted into the clear blue skies, my mind raced with doubts about whether I had made the right decision to leave my homeland. What was my destiny and what kind of challenges would I face? I looked at my wife and daughter and wondered whether I was taking the right course of action for them. My face betrayed my anxiety and fear of the unknown, but deep inside, I knew that it was the best I could do for us.

The six-hour flight to Honolulu, Hawaii, was uneventful. During the two-hour layover, we took a stroll through the terminal. We bought two ham sandwiches and two Pepsis—and the bill came to nineteen US dollars. My wife and I looked at one another and thought that it was the most expensive lunch we had ever bought and wondered whether the prices were going to be the same on the mainland. In Fiji, the same lunch would have cost us less than eight dollars. My mind was bogged down by the idea that, because we were going to be making big money in America, a nineteen-dollar lunch would be just pocket change. I kept reminding myself that it wouldn't be long before we could afford to live in a big luxurious house, drive a big Chevy, and have a big savings account. Little did I know that it would take years of hard work and a lot of sacrifices to achieve these material things and to live the American Dream of luxury and prosperity.

We got back on our plane and, in six hours, we arrived in San Francisco. My parents, my two brothers, my sister, and brother-in-law were waiting for us at the terminal. We exchanged hugs, kisses, and stories. We waited for our luggage, collected it, loaded into my father's Monte Carlo, and were off to my parents' home in Oakland.

They had a modest home decorated with American-style furniture—and lots of family pictures on the walls. My parents were overjoyed to see us after several years of only phone calls and letters. They were delighted to feast their eyes on their first granddaughter. We were welcomed with a chicken curry dinner and traditional rice, daal, chutney, and lots of other savories that my mother and sister had cooked earlier in the day. We had cocktails and thoroughly enjoyed my mother's delicious food.

It was well after midnight before we went to bed. I got up the next morning and it was already ten o' clock. The beautiful winter morning was cold, but the skies were clear and blue. It warmed up quite a bit during the midday, making me feel as if I had the made the right decision to move to the Bay Area. Watching children play in the streets was a first for me. In my old country, while growing up, we never played on the road. We always had plenty of space in our backyard or in neighborhood parks to play with our friends. The other first was the way that the roads and streets were planned, designed, and built. Everything—from houses to fences to driveways, and gutters—looked clean and showed pride of ownership.

I realized—to my amazement—that all the vehicles were driving on the right side. I started to wonder whether I would ever be able to drive on the right side, but after speaking with my folks, I was assured that it would be an easy transition. The other thing that took me by surprise was that I noticed an equal number of male and female drivers. At that point, I reminded myself that this was a land of equal opportunity. Women had equality—and enjoyed astronomical socioeconomic advances.

With each passing day, slowly but surely, the culture shock started to set in. Change and adjustment were the code words. Everywhere I looked—TV, roads, parks, shopping centers, and movie theatres—the demeanor and lifestyle and thinking of American people were different. They spoke differently, they dressed differently, and they had slightly different opinions about life and how to live it. I immediately realized that there were some things that I would have to learn in order to quickly adjust to American lifestyle.

Over a few weeks, it occurred to me that there were a bunch of things that I could read about, learn, and practice immediately. In doing so, my daily living—and my chances of obtaining my first job—would become easier. I sat down and made a list. The more inquisitive I got and the more that I watched the way others were carrying on with their daily lives, the longer my list grew. My father and brothers were my mentors and assisted me in compiling it. My list included:

1. Obtaining a driver's license. Without a driver's license, it would be just about impossible to get a job. I had to get driving lessons and go for a driving test. Once my license was obtained, I had to get a decent, reliable car.

2. Obtaining a Social Security card. Without one, I was told that no employer would want to even interview me. We went to the Social Security office and were told that the card would arrive in the mail in six weeks. It actually only took five.

3. Obtaining health insurance. I was informed that medical insurance was also a necessity because, if one of us got sick, I would have to spend virtually all of my money on medical bills. Since I was a spiritual person, I prayed every day that none of us would get sick until I got a job and was enrolled in a medical insurance plan.

4. Learning American English. I needed to quickly learn clear American English so that everyone would understand me. I had always spoken fluent English, but I had a strong East Indian accent. To remedy this, I tried to listen to more English radio stations and TV programs. When I was alone, I repeated sentences and phrases to myself. I was determined to get the American style of pronunciation. I was strongly advised to get familiar with some American slang. Some of the words that I quickly learned were:

   - *Bent* means angry
   - *Bombed* means intoxicated

- *Cool* means good
- *Couch potato* means lazy person
- *Dork* means strange person
- *Dough* means money
- *Grub* means food
- *Screw up* means to make mistakes
- *Sucker* means a person who is deceived easily
- *Goofy* means silly
- *Hang* loose means to relax
- *John* means bathroom
- *Make waves* means to cause trouble
- *Flaky* means unreliable
- *Faucet* means tap
- *Cans* mean tins
- *To go* means take-away

The list had another hundred words—some of which I still do not know. I was also told about American spellings that were different from British. I was told there were many words that were spelled without the letter *u* in them, such as *labor, honor, color*, etc.

5. Opening a checking account. I was advised to immediately open a checking account. My father took me to a bank down the road from his house, and I opened a checking account. I was advised to pay for all my transactions with checks. In the old country, cash transactions were very common—especially for ordinary daily commodities. At the same time, I had to quickly learn what a quarter, nickel, and dime looked like. We had to familiarize ourselves with these coins. We had not been familiar with these currency terms. We were used to pound, shilling, and pence.

6. Learning local sports. During my first weekend in America, my two younger brothers, Arvind and Pravin

Balram, introduced me to local sports. I was told that I had to learn the rules and regulations relating to American football and baseball. I grew up playing soccer and rugby and had no idea why one nation would have so much passion for American football and baseball.

7. Locking all doors and windows. I was cautioned that one must keep all doors and windows of the house—and car—locked at all times. This was for my personal security and protection and to secure my property. In the old country, we left everything open all the time since robbery and burglary were very seldom encountered.

8. Obeying police officers. While discussing the security issues, I was also informed that all police officers—and some security guards—carried weapons. One should not disobey their orders—no matter how unreasonable their demands.

9. Carrying identification. I was further advised to carry a photo ID with me at all times. You never know when a peace officer may stop you and ask for a valid identification card. This is a normal practice when one is suspected of committing some sort of crime—no matter how petty.

10. Learning opposites. It did not take me long to find out that dates were written differently than the British system; light switches operated in the opposite way; and doors opened in the opposite direction. Power currents were AC and not DC; you had to tip in restaurants and did not have to dress up while going to movies or restaurants. The list of minor differences was endless.

11. Preparing a résumé. Most importantly, for employment opportunities, it was a necessity to prepare a résumé. In the old country, we had to just call a potential employer and try to get an interview—or someone knew someone and would set up an interview for you. Thus, preparing a résumé and sending it to potential employers was new for me. Since finding a job was my top priority, I hurriedly found my father's old typewriter and—with the help of my wife, who happened to be a good typist—I was able to put a résumé together. We went to the library, found a photocopy machine, and I made several dozen copies. I went through the Yellow Pages and looked up the names of all the attorneys in the area. For the next several weeks, I mailed at least one hundred résumés to different law offices seeking a job in any capacity. Since we did not have computers or the Internet in those days, I just waited for the phone to ring. Over the next few weeks, a few potential employers called and promised to get back, but I never heard from them again.

After a month or so, I landed a very good job in a small law office as a law clerk. One of the partners took me under his tutelage and taught me about American jurisprudence, the American system of law, and American court procedures.

Over the next few years, I spent much of my spare time in law libraries, teaching myself the American legal system. It was difficult and often frustrating, but I had to pass the bar exams—and that compelled me to keep studying at every opportunity.

With these newly learnt lessons, I thought that I was ready to tackle the stress and tensions of daily living, but I was far from being anywhere close to ready. Not only was I somewhat confused about the whole new culture, I was extremely concerned about how I was going to balance my own culture and religion with American lifestyle and culture. The thought that gave me some relief was that I was going to take the best from American culture and try to assimilate it with my own East Indian culture and traditions. I became more determined to learn all about my new adopted country—its history and many wonderful traditions. I told myself that I was going to be cautious—and I did not have to take everything at its face value. I was going to look at new things with an open, fair, impartial mind and then utilize the things that were going to benefit me the most. I was going to keep all my options open. The thought that kept me content was that I was a young, energetic, well-educated, and open-minded person. I consoled myself with my belief that it would not be difficult for me to assimilate. Although some of my values, aspirations, dreams, and ideas were adverse to what I was seeing and experiencing in my new country, I always felt confident that with the passing of time, new employment, financial security, a nice home, and cars, things would turn favorably for me. Sooner or later, I knew that we would become the beneficiaries of the American Dream.

The reality set in and it was time to execute my plans. Lots of energy and passion were now required to proceed full steam ahead. I kept on telling myself that hard work, drive, and determination would take me to the zenith. There was no looking back. There was no need to have any second thoughts. I was living in the greatest country on earth and, if I could not make myself successful, prosperous, happy, wealthy, and content, there was no other place that I could find contentment and happiness.

The famous speech of Hindu philosopher Swami Vivekananda reverberated in my mind. More than a hundred years ago, the great scholar of Hinduism gave a remarkable speech while in America on a world tour.

We are responsible for what we are and whatever we wish ourselves to be, we have the power to make ourselves. If what we are now has been the result of our past actions, it certainly follows that whatever we wish to be in the future can be produced by our present actions; so, we do have to know how to act wisely no matter where we live.

This speech reminded me that I could become someone in America and leave my mark, but I would have to work very hard and think wisely in order to achieve the American Dream. I looked around and found hundreds of immigrant friends and relatives doing very well financially, socially, and spiritually, adjusting well to the American way of life. There was no reason why I could not do the same.

Chapter 2:
Your First Job

"Happiness lies in being privileged to work hard for long hours in doing whatever you think is worth doing. One man may find happiness in supporting his wife and children by digging ditches. Another may find happiness in robbing banks. Still another may labor mightily for years in doing pure research with no discernable results. Thus, no two are alike and there is no reason to expect them to be. Each man must find himself that occupation in which hard work and long hours makes him happy. Counter wise, if you are looking for shorter hours and longer vacations and early retirement then you need to take up robbing banks or get in a side show or even politics."

—Robert Heinlein

They call America "the land of opportunity", and for centuries the United States has lived up to that motto. People from all over the world come to these shores seeking a better way of life for themselves and their families. The streets are not paved with gold as the quaint old saying once mused. Nevertheless, America offers something more precious than gold: opportunity. A nation founded by and built by immigrants, the United States has fostered

11

a culture that appreciates the contributions of anyone who wants to come here to pursue their dreams. That might mean opening a small business, getting a great education, or going to work for a huge corporation. All are given an equal chance to showcase their talents and give life their best effort. It is a wealthy and prosperous nation, with enough goods and services for all who are willing to work hard for them.

However, nobody starts at the top. How many times have you heard that highly educated and qualified people from other countries when they first migrate to America have to take menial work just to survive? Some work in fast-food places and some become taxi drivers and others work in manufacturing—toiling away in factories and warehouses. A good percentage of these immigrants have degrees in liberal arts, science, law, or business, but they have no experience working in America. They have no work references to show a potential employer that they have worked for someone in America. There is nothing to write on their résumés about their work history and experience in the United States. This is a major hurdle that one must overcome in order to get that crucial first job. (By the way, there is nothing wrong with doing insignificant types of work in order to support yourself and your family. Honesty, integrity, and hard work are what count.)

The bad news is that the establishment and development of one's career in the United States start at the bottom of the ladder. No doubt that there are some exceptions. Some new immigrants have good contacts and networks, received an excellent education abroad, and are able to find suitable work quickly. Some are sponsored by large corporations to come to this country and work for them because no equally qualified person could be found here. But, then one still has to learn to do things according to the American way. Employers want their employees to do things according to tried and proven American ways.

The general rule of thumb is that one has to start at the bottom of the ladder proving one's education, training, and experience at every step of the way. Employers are usually quick to recognize their employees' abilities. As long as one is a productive worker and has the drive, determination, and desire to make progress, employers have no hesitation in promoting their good employees. I have found that once you have proven that you are a reliable, hardworking, loyal employee, your employer begins to trust and respect you. That is when an employer starts to give you more responsibilities. With more responsibilities come more pay and more benefits.

Just as in any other country, if one is desirous to have a high quality of life and a great career, a good education is crucial. In this great country, the more educated and qualified a person is, the more limitless is his horizon. He can ask for a fair and going rate of salary and can move from one region to the other depending on where he wants to live and work.

The question is how a well-educated immigrant can quickly mainstream into the American work environment? One of the first things that a new immigrant must consider is whether he is in need of more education. Self-assessment is very important. If you think that you need more training and education, then that is where to start. If one can afford a few years of college education or training in the technical school of one's choosing, then it should be seriously considered. Obviously, it would entail a lot of stress, tension, and overwhelming demands on your time, strength, and finances, but in the long run, it will all be worth it. Once this initial education in an American school system has been accomplished, then finding a good job and living a great life should not be difficult. There is little doubt that if you want to advance and prosper rapidly, you need to have a bona fide certificate from an American school. How you will finance your education will be a major hurdle, but there are always student loans, scholarships, sponsorships, and other sources of funds that should be explored. It is not going to be easy, especially for those who have a young family, but it can be done. Once you find financing, you have to think about how you are going to support your family, especially if your spouse is not working and there are young children. Taking part- time jobs, working from home, and living on a limited budget will have to be seriously considered. Tension, stress, and frustrations will have to be kept in check. Major sacrifices will have to be made.

The other way of getting acclimatized to the American work environment is to ask your potential employer if you can work for a few hours a day in their establishment with no pay. A small percentage of employers will be agreeable. This way, you will get to learn how things are done and get to know a few nice people who will be able to help you learn the tricks of the trade. There is always that possibility that if you are able to prove yourself as a somewhat qualified person to accept a position, then if an opening does occur, you can make a request to be considered for that position.

The first job is always the hardest to find. You are competing with so many qualified people who probably have more experience and training than you do. The whole idea should be to focus on getting your foot in the door.

It would be a good idea to devise a plan. Package yourself and ask yourself whether the job would be easy to do or learn and whether it is what you want to do for the rest of your life. Thereafter, decide what type of jobs you would like to interview for based on your education and qualifications and maybe some type of related experience. Maybe you do not have a choice and have to grab the first offer—it all depends on your financial situation.

It will not be easy to get your first job. You need lady luck, good credentials, and a personality that gets recognized immediately by a potential employer. Initially, it may seem impossible to get that job that you studied so hard for. Do not get disappointed. Keep your focus on your ultimate goal. Disappointments and failures usually open some other door. Winners always explore their opportunities. Learn to adapt, dream, invert, and innovate.

Prepare dozens of résumés and send them to as many employers as you can. Ask friends and family members for names and addresses of potential employers. Go through the telephone directories. Look for companies on the Internet that may interest you. Major companies have a section showing careers or openings. Browse and take notes. Just keep on mailing or e-mailing those résumés. Networking with friends and relatives will all help. If your English language skills are good, do not be scared to make phone calls to human resources departments and find out whether they have any openings. When rejections start coming in, don't be alarmed. It is part of the game plan to find a job. If you start to worry about rejections, it will only undermine your self-confidence. Sooner or later, you will be granted an interview. Thereafter, you will have to learn how to succeed in giving a good interview. This can also be learned. There are books in the local libraries and career counselors who can coach you how to give great job interviews. Some of these learning services can be obtained for free. Call your local employment office and employment development department run by the state. They will be happy to teach you a few good interview tricks. You may want to contact a career counselor. Temporary hiring service agencies will also provide you lots of training and advice. Many large corporations now recruit primarily from temp agencies. Go to these temp agencies, take tests, and see how good you are. They will want to train you and get you hired. Temp agencies make good commissions for screening and providing efficient and productive employees.

Once you get an interview date, start learning about the company where you have been called for an interview. The more you get to know about your potential employer, the more you can impress your interviewer about your interest and passion to work for their company. You have to remember that an interviewer wants to hire people who they think will be able to do the job. Secondly, they look for someone who will become productive in a very short time and thirdly, a person who will get along with other employees. At the interview, sell yourself. Show the interviewer how you can help the company grow and thrive. Show enthusiasm by participating in the conversation. Ask some pertinent questions and show positive body language.

These days, employers also want to see in any prospective employee that they have good communication skills. This means the ability to speak and to write well. Also be willing to listen. Show them that you are a self-starter. Employers do not want to have to tell you each and everything to do. You must be prepared to be innovative and use your imagination. Since employers look for people with good people skills, remember to be friendly, respectful, and courteous with your customers.

Also, be aware that many employers these days will want to check your credit report. They just want to see if an employee is an honest, responsible, and ethical person. You have to say yes to this request. If you want to work for banking or financial institutions, you will have to allow the potential employer to check your credit. If your credit is not all that good, then there are ways to explain this. You should bring this issue up on your own and explain it by giving a few good reasons why your credit is spotty or why it is not fully established. Since you are new to the country, the employer will understand.

The job-seeking task is a job in itself. Some experts say that a person should spend at least forty hours per week looking for that first job. Write, e-mail, phone, make contacts, network, read about potential companies that you want to work for, and consult with professionals. Destiny and good luck play a small part in searching for that first job. Good qualifications, training, enthusiasm, and good interview techniques play a major role.

The other advice is to stay positive. We all need strength to pursue our dreams. You must not quit. The American economy is not too robust right now. Unemployment is hovering at about 12 percent nationwide. The average person with average qualifications spends up to seven months of persistent job searching to find that crucial first job. Keep your self-esteem high. Keep in good health. Your spirit and morale are important too. If you think that you are a loser, you will definitely lose, but if you think you are a winner, you will win. You are what you think. Sooner or later, the phone will ring. If you have tried hard to search for that desired job and lady luck is on your side, you will get the job.

CHAPTER 3:
YOUR FIRST CAR

It has been said that Americans have a love affair with automobiles. Just look around almost anywhere in the United States and you will see just how true that is. There are cars, trucks, motorcycles, and SUVs of every size, shape, and color. All of the nation's major cities—not to mention just about every suburb and small town—are linked together by a vast and intricate network of paved interstate highways, roadways, boulevards, and streets.

Perhaps because America is such a large nation (the fourth largest in land area in the entire world), the people love the idea of being able to get from point A to point B whenever they want quickly and efficiently. What once would take days by horseback can now be traversed in a matter of hours by automobile. Americans have even made life as convenient as possible by having drive-through restaurants, banks, etc. Clearly, the automobile has become an integral feature of modern American life.

For these reasons and more, ownership of a nice, reliable vehicle is going to be a very important aspect of your life once you arrive in this country. American society is very mobile and a good means of transportation is of utmost importance. It is like an "internal passport." One will need a good reliable vehicle to find a job, to run your errands, to go shopping, for visiting, for commuting to work, for identification purposes and also, a nice vehicle exhibits your social status and lifestyle. An average American spends seventy-two minutes per weekday in transit either going or coming from work, grocery shopping, or running errands. The average American household spends approximately $5,477 on gas and other auto-related expenses per year—and that does not include payment of a car loan. In some states, this figure could be as high as $7,600. Owning a car is not something that should be taken lightly. It could put a big dent in your monthly income.

Buying your first car will be the first major investment that one will have to think about very seriously. It may be an expensive car that you are interested in or it may be just an ordinary, simple car that you merely want for necessary transportation to and from work and for weekend running around. What you decide will depend on how much money you want to spend on the car and for how long you plan to keep it. It's also important to know how much you want the car to reflect your lifestyle. Some people have fancy vehicles to boost their egos and display pride of ownership. Others are anxious to display how prosperous they are to their friends and relatives; some people are car enthusiasts and want to own fast cars to satisfy their own fantasies.

If you are going to buy a new car from a dealer, then there is not much that you have to do. As long as you like the car and have decided on the price and the dealer can get you a loan, everything should go smoothly. However, you have to be very careful that the dealer does not quote an outrageous price for the car. The first car that you own in this country will be your most expensive asset and investment. It will have to be reasonably priced and you must be happy with the monthly payments.

Buying a used car can be a risky transaction. Since most new immigrants buy used cars first, there are certain things to consider. How will you use the vehicle? How long do you plan to keep it? Will the payments fit into your monthly budget? You will have to factor in maintenance and insurance costs as well. Auto insurance is mandatory in most states and that is another commodity that one can shop around for. Different companies will give different premium quotes. A person's driving record and experience will be factored in when an agent provides an insurance quote.

Whatever source you use to find a car that you like, you must investigate and compare prices before making an offer. The Kelly Blue Book and similar car-valuation sources should be consulted. This can all be done on the Internet. You can also consult friends and relatives who have been in this country for a while. It is important to know the ballpark price of the car that you are interested in buying.

You can also buy good used cars from new car dealers. These vehicles are usually in good condition, but are slightly more expensive. They are trade-ins that were taken when a buyer bought a new car, and likely come with a warranty under which the dealer is obligated to fix problems during the warranty period. Sometimes the warranty will be good for two years. Of course, extra money has to be paid for extended warranties.

Most used cars are purchased from used car dealers. These cars usually have more mileage and are in worse shape than what the new car dealers have to offer. Always ask for warranties on these used cars. Some of the dealers are unscrupulous and will sell you a piece of junk. Americans call such vehicles "lemons."

Car rental agencies also sell used cars. These vehicles are well maintained and service records are readily available. However, the disadvantage is that mileage on these cars is higher on a per-year basis. Some banks also have used cars that they want to sell. These are repossessed cars and the quality will vary from car to car.

There are also private owners who sell their cars. These are usually advertised in newspapers, as well as on eBay and other places on the Internet. Most of them are reasonably priced and sellers are anxious to sell. The disadvantage of buying these cars from private owners is that no warranty is provided by the seller and there are usually no maintenance records. You must be extra careful when buying from a private owner. A thorough inspection and a good road test are very important. Listen for engine noise. Check out things such as tires, lights, shock absorbers, and body alignment. The safest way to buy a used car is to take it to a mechanic to have it checked out. For a small fee, any repair shop will take a look at the car. The technician will provide a report and then you can decide what to do. Automobile associations such as the Automobile Association of America (AAA) can also conduct a thorough check of used cars for their members.

The bottom line is to be extra careful when purchasing a used car. Be careful what interest rate is offered for a car loan and be careful not to buy a car that will require too much gas to run, too much maintenance, too much space to park, too much insurance to keep, or too many hassles to own. The fancier the car, the more hassle in parking and garaging. It may also drain a chunk of your monthly income.

I recall buying my first car; I had to spend almost a full day with the used car dealer. We had some problems in getting a loan, but it eventually came through. The loan department usually wants to verify your wages, look at your credit history, look at the down payment, and your monthly budget. Sometimes you have to go to your own bank to obtain financing. Others have their friends or relatives finance them. Whatever the source, any car loan should be in writing and all the terms and conditions should be clearly written.

The one thing that I vividly remember about buying my first used car, which was a six-year-old Toyota Corolla wagon that I paid $1,800 for, was that the car salesman shook my hand and reminded me never to drink and drive. What a wonderful piece of advice that was. It reminded me of a joke. A policeman stopped a motorist for driving erratically. He peered into the driver's eyes and said, "Your eyes look bloodshot. Have you been drinking?"

The driver peered intently into the police officer's eyes and said, "Your eyes look glazed, have you been eating doughnuts?"

It is important to own a reliable vehicle in this country. Public transportation is not all that good in America, so you need your own set of wheels. Once you obtain a driver's license and a vehicle, you can say that you are on track to achieving the American Dream. Cruising on the beautiful freeways and having the freedom to go anywhere at any time will make you feel as if you are the king of the road. However, always keep in mind that driving is a privilege. Your safety and the safety of others should be of paramount consideration. Abide by the traffic laws and never drink and drive. If you get caught, it will mean huge fines, maybe some jail time, and suspension of driving privileges. The first driving under the influence ticket can set you back as much as $7,000 if you decide to get an attorney.

Thus, it is very important to always remember that driving under the influence of any substance or alcohol will bring financial ruin, shame, and punishment to you as well as to your family. Once you get caught drinking and driving, everyone in the family is affected.

CHAPTER 4:
YOUR FIRST APARTMENT

Most new arrivals in the United States will not have enough money to buy a home right away. In all likelihood, the new immigrant will need to first rent an apartment or condominium. While living there, if you manage your finances wisely, you will ideally be able to someday put aside enough of a down payment to purchase a home of your own.

But, first things first. No matter how much love and affection or financial security that may be forthcoming from your parents, relatives, or friends while you initially live with them, it is always nice to find your own place, especially if you are married and have children. Parents, friends, and relatives need space. They are entitled to live according to their own lifestyle. Responsible adults have to realize that the sooner they can move out on their own, the quicker they can build their own foundation to live independently. With these thoughts in mind, my wife and I decided to find our own little apartment. We had one small income. We had to find a place that did not consume the bulk of our monthly budget. When we started looking, we were advised that our application would have to show the source of our income and the amount per month. We were told to be ready to pay two months' rent in advance—plus a few hundred dollars for a cleaning deposit.

We started to make appointments and to inspect the apartments near my job in Livermore, California. It did not take us long to find a place that we liked. We filled out the application and were told that our credit history and employment would have to be verified. We were told to wait a week for the answer. We kept our fingers crossed for a favorable response. Within a week, we got the good news that we could have the apartment—provided we had a cosigner. Once again, we had to implore our parents to be the savior and they obliged.

The next hurdle was buying some basic furniture. Since we had to come up with money up front to get the apartment, we were essentially broke. We were used to having some nice furniture in our apartment back in the old country, but the issue of affording decent furniture loomed large. We decided to just get two beds and a small dining table. My daughter already had her crib that my parents had bought. My parents also gave us some furniture of their own. We hired a small U-Haul and were able to move everything in one trip. My brothers and my brother-in-law helped with the heavy lifting.

Whilst the move out from my parents' house was a bit emotional and they felt really and truly sad to see us leave, they realized and understood that I was anxious to stand on my own feet. The new country, new environment, new job, new social circle, new ideas, and new thoughts were all having a positive effect on me. They did not want to disrupt my progress. I felt good about the fact that I was slowly getting onto my feet, getting to know my freedoms, and taking advantage of them.

When we first moved into our new apartment, I did not like that we had to keep all the windows and doors of the apartment closed, especially at nighttime. In the old country, we were used to leaving our windows open. We were also having a hard time sleeping without mosquito nets. Over the years, we had become used to sleeping within the confines of the mosquito net.

Without the mosquito net, it took us a long time to fall asleep every night. A good habit is usually hard to break and this was a good, healthy habit that we had to get rid of. Slowly, but surely, we got used to sleeping without our nets. The other thing that we had to adjust to was taking hot showers. In the old country, the colder the water, the more refreshing the bath was. The idea of washing and cleaning in hot water was hygienic, but it took us some time to get used to. Having lived in a tropical country virtually all my life where there was no need of a hot water supply, it was difficult for us to shower—even on a cold day—with hot water. But, we slowly became accustomed to this ritual.

A few things to keep in mind before leasing an apartment:

- Your budget should play an essential role in the type and location of the apartment. Try to get your first apartment close to your work. You should not spend more than 35 percent of your income on rent. If you live in an expensive city, you might have to pay up to 50 percent of your income toward rent.
- A typical apartment includes one bedroom and one bathroom; floor plans range from 750–900 square feet. It should come with a refrigerator, stove, and dishwasher. Some of them will have a washer, dryer, and a built-in microwave oven.
- Apartment owners usually charge a certain amount of money as a security deposit (often one month's rent) and they may ask for a small deposit for cleaning. Always ask who will be responsible

for paying for utilities, such as water, electricity, and garbage pick-up. All of these things should be specifically mentioned in the lease.

- The lease should mention things such as the term of the lease, who will pay for breakdowns in plumbing or electrical systems, and who will be responsible for maintaining any lawns or gardens.

- Once the lease is signed, the tenant should complete a move-in checklist about the condition of the walls, and appliances. Take photographs of each room. Doing so will make it easier to get your security and cleaning deposits back at the termination of the lease.

- If you can afford to buy tenant's insurance, it would be very wise thing to do. That way, if there is a fire, burglary, or some other calamity, your possessions, such as furniture, jewelry, and appliances, will be covered. Your landlord's insurance will not cover your personal items and possessions.

The idea behind having your first apartment is to establish your independence. Everyone yearns for his or her own space. The idea of getting on your feet and establishing your own lifestyle with your own decorations, furniture, and standard of cleanliness is very satisfying. A man's home is his castle—no matter how small, dirty, or decrepit it may be. These days, there are plenty of apartments available for rent in any neighborhood. The length of your search will depend on how much time you want to devote toward driving around and looking for a nice unit. It will depend on how far you want to commute to work. Keep things such as wear and tear on your car and money spent on gas and tolls in mind when searching for an apartment. You must also make sure that the landlord is providing you with a clean, safe, and secure place. It is the landlord's responsibility to make sure that the apartment is fit for human habitability: a roof that does not leak, windows that close properly, carpet that is clean, and walls that are painted and clean. Check out the neighborhood before you sign the lease. Drive around the neighborhood at nighttime to find out if there is gang activity, homeless people hanging around, drugs or alcohol being sold, or police handling traffic and family disputes.

Get a safe, secure, quiet place where you can live without hassles. It reminds me of a joke when a prospective tenant was inspecting an apartment. The tenant heard a noise like a mouse eating something and said, "I did not expect to hear a mouse in a new apartment." The owner, after taking a deep breath, replied, "That's not a mouse; the man next door is eating celery."

CHAPTER 5:
THE UNIQUENESS OF THE UNITED STATES

Americans have always thought of their country as a unique place in the world. In fact, some of its earliest patriots extolled its virtues as being like a "shining city upon a hill." In other words, the United States likes to see itself as a beacon of hope and freedom to the rest of the world—ideals that are personified by the famous Statue of Liberty. What is it that makes America so different from all of the other nations on this planet?

As soon as you arrive in this country, you realize that the United States has some unique features. It does not matter how many countries you have visited in the past, how many travel magazines you have read, or how many friends or relatives you have spoken with about the description America—it is certainly different in more than one way from other countries. The United States definitely can boast of some unique governmental, geographical, cultural, and structural features. This is what initially amazed me about America. The roads and freeways were different, the architecture was different, the pace of life was different, the thinking of its people was different, and myriad other things are done differently here. I had to do some reading and researching to find out why the United States has clung to its unique features. Once you understand them, you will realize that the founding fathers really had in mind to create a "new country" different from anywhere else on this earth. Its uniqueness is one of the reasons why Americans are so proud of their nation and patriotism is close to the heart of its citizens. One only has to observe the celebrations during the Fourth of July (Independence Day) to notice how proud and appreciative Americans are of their country. The country has many features that are unique when compared with any country in Europe—even Great Britain from where the founding fathers originally hailed. This is just one of the reasons why many immigrants, especially the young folks, are so desirous to come to this country. They want to experience something new—a new system of governance, unique geography, scenery, and lifestyle.

The Uniqueness of the American Constitution

The United States constitution has to be most unique document in the entire world. In 1787 Americans gave the world the first example of a written constitution for the operation of its democratic government. This document is still the backbone that allows America to be an example of freedom and righteousness. The United States constitution allows its citizens the basic freedom that any human being deserves and does not infringe on one's individuality. It protects its citizens economically, religiously, politically and socially.

The American constitution is careful in defining where certain power lies for state and federal governments. The states hold just enough power to keep the federal government from having complete control. For example, the federal government holds exclusive powers to control militia and foreign relations. The states have no say in these powers reserved in the federal government. For example, if each state had its own army and its own foreign policy, the idea of being " united" would be meaningless. This would only be a lip service and the entire country will have fifty or so different foreign policies.

The three branches of the federal government, that is, executive, judicial and legislative has defined powers and no branch has more power than another. This division of power and the fact that Congress is made up of so many elected representatives, gives the general public a very active role in the government. Since the idea is to let the people rule themselves, American government cannot infringe on many of the choices that its citizens makes. Due to the Bill of Rights, citizens have the right to say, hear, write and be anywhere they wish to be. Also, due to the division of powers in the federal government, the threat of dictatorship is non- existent in America. The Constitution states, "We the People", which is what makes this document and America so unique.

Geographic Features

By looking at the US map, you will notice that the borders of the nation are broken. Alaska, which happens to be the biggest state in the country, is separated (by Canada) from the mainland. This is a somewhat unusual geographic alignment of a country. Non–contiguous enclaves of this sort create security and logistical problems for the national government. That is the reason why some Canadians often joke that Alaska should belong to Canadians. It is in their neighborhood and shares many geographical features.

The Capital District

The capital of the country, Washington DC is not a part of any state of the union. Washington is situated in the District of Columbia— not in a specific state. This gives Washington a neutral status. The residents do not have any representation in Congress (which, by the way, is an issue of some controversy).

Residents of Washington have just one delegate to represent them. Few other countries have this type of political set-up, but their residents are given the power to vote for their representative to the national government. A good example of this is Australia.

No Official Language

English is still not the official language of the United States—despite the fact that most Americans only speak English. Almost all business is conducted in English. It has to be noted that nearly thirty states have passed legislation to make English the official language. Furthermore, state and federal governments are obliged to provide various services in more than a dozen different languages upon request, but English has not been adopted as the country's official language. There is a strong political movement to make English the official language, but it will take some time. Spanish is widely spoken and fast becoming the second most widely used language. Becoming bilingual is highly encouraged in the United States; in some occupations, it is easier to get jobs if one is bilingual.

Imperial System

The United States is one of a few countries that use the Imperial system for weights and measurements. While most countries have converted to the metric system, the United States continues to calculate measurements in ounces, pounds, gallons, inches, feet, and yards. Everyone coming from the metric system countries will have to be educated about this archaic system of measurement. There is a movement to change this, but the government is not very interested in adopting the metric system. I guess that it will happen in the very near future because the rest of the world finds the metric system a more sensible and easier method to measure and weigh things.

The Central Bank

The bank of the United States is called the Federal Reserve Bank of the United States. The agency of the government is responsible for augmenting sound monetary policies. In other countries, the central government bank is named after the country, i.e. the Bank of England.

The Electoral College

This is a unique system. In any presidential election, the members of the college play a crucial role. Other countries allow the voters to elect a president directly by popular votes, but not in America. The president has to be elected by electoral college members known as electors. Each state elects a certain number of electors to the college, based on the state's population. These electoral college members (electors) vote to choose the president. If the members of the college do not want to make a person president, they can deprive that right to a person who has obtained the majority of popular votes.

The National Anthem

This is another thing that fascinates me about this country. America's national anthem, "The Star-Spangled Banner," does not mention the United States or America anywhere in the lyrics. Most countries' national anthems mention the name of the country somewhere. I hope that this can be changed one day, but so far, there has been no hue and cry to do this.

The Ownership of Firearms

It amazed me when I first arrived in this country and was told about the number of people who owned guns and had the right to do so. This right is given to its citizens by the Constitution. It is estimated that 40 percent of American households have at least one gun. In fact, there are more privately owned firearms in the United States than in any other country—both per capita and in total. The United States is the most-armed country in the world. American citizens argue that they have to own the guns to defend themselves, but guns are also kept for hunting, plinking, and target shooting. These are some of the hobbies that American citizens enjoy. The proliferation of guns creates a lot of social problems and volumes of violent crimes, but the citizens have this right. Every time there is major cry from the electorate to ban guns, the gun lobbyists spend millions of dollars to defeat it and politicians shy away from this controversy.

There are numerous other unique things embedded in the American systems, traditions, and cultures. One will notice special festivities during the first year of their stay in this country. Halloween, which has evolved from an ancient Celtic festival, is widely celebrated by young and old. Children go from door to door saying "Trick or Treat" in exchange for candies. Elders stay home and party. Some cities have Halloween street fairs.

Independence Day (Fourth of July) and Thanksgiving (last Thursday in November) are also popular festivals in this country and are celebrated with parades, sports, and pomp—unlike anywhere else in this world.

Having a little knowledge about these unique features will only enhance an immigrant's understanding of American style of governance and democracy. The United States is, in many ways, different from other countries. That is why the United States is sometimes referred to as the "last best hope of earth", a phrase that was coined by President Abraham Lincoln in 1862 and it still rings so true.

Whether they immigrated from Mexico, Philippines, India, Japan, China, Iran, Nigeria, Ukraine, Italy, Ireland, Germany,

Sweden, Scotland or England, all immigrants believed that the pursuit of happiness has got to be their goal. They lived and worked shoulder to shoulder for many years and still continue to do, unifying the sense of their American identity. The end result being, these people from different countries and background have created a unique society with its own unique culture, customs and traditions.

CHAPTER 6:
CULTURE SHOCK AND ASSIMILATION

"Assimilation does not mean repudiating an immigrant's culture. It is much more flexible and accommodating. Consequently, much more effective in achieving its purpose to allow the US to preserve its national unity in the face of the influx of hordes of persons of scores of different nationalities."

—Henry Fairchild

Every immigrant who comes to America faces a dilemma. They want to become Americans, to assimilate into the society and culture of the United States, and basically blend in with everyone else. On the other hand, we want to retain our heritage and pass it on to our children. We want to both take on a new identity and, at the same time, remain true to our ancestors. It is fine line that every immigrant must learn how to walk.

If you want to be successful in a career and have a positive impact on neighbors, friends, and co-workers, you must strive to assimilate and become familiar with the cultures, values, and traditions of American society. Immigrants must identify themselves as Americans, placing that identity ahead of their motherland. America is the great melting pot, but there are certain recipes that must be savored in order to get the full flavor of goodies emanating from the pot. It is important that an immigrant must have some knowledge and appreciation of the adopted country's traditions and culture. Not everything that the adopted country may offer will be beneficial, but the negative things can be ignored. However, we can learn many good things from native-born Americans. The liberal ideologies propounded by the Constitution, the American commitment to build its economy based on free market capitalism, and the wide infatuation that Americans have for philanthropic gestures make it easier for immigrants to assimilate and be accepted by people who were born and raised in America. The recent upward trend of intercultural marriages and allowing immigrants to take on key positions in corporations and in the public sector shows that native-born Americans are willing to embrace immigrants.

The United States has the largest population of immigrants in the world. A recent estimate shows that over 38.5 million people living in the United States are first generation immigrants. On an annual basis, the United States naturalizes approximately 898,000 immigrants as new citizens, the most of any country in the world. Thus, it is only fair and reasonable for the new immigrants to at least, try and learn some of the norms and traditions of the "American Spirit" which will in due course give you that American identity. An American identity does not mean that you totally have to forget your own culture but it will make you a proud American living the American dream.; it gives you an identity to be counted as one of the "Yankees". Even adopting on an informal basis, an American nick name like, Andy, Rob, Chris or Trudy, Becky, Betty would not hurt. Americans like abbreviated names. It is easier to remember.

Assimilation occurs when an immigrant absorbs the cultural norms, values, and behavior patterns of the host society, including learning English and becoming a naturalized American citizen. You can retain much of your traditional culture while acquiring American social ways. One type of assimilation is the socioeconomic assimilation that occurs when an immigrant completely immerses himself into the formal social, political, economic, and cultural institutions of the host country.

If you look around, you will find that some racial and ethnic groups assimilate faster than others do. Why is this? Is one racial group more anxious to become Americanized than the other is? There are different reasons for this. One factor is the racial differences. For example, the white immigrants who came to the United States in the 1800s certainly experienced prejudices, but because they were white, they were able to integrate into American society more quickly and easily than non-white immigrants were.

The second factor is the structure of the economy. During times of economic prosperity, there are plenty of opportunities for everyone. However, in times of economic hardships, there is more competition. This means more hostility toward immigrants and minorities since they are seen as threats for jobs, housing, and other socioeconomic resources.

The third reason why some immigrants assimilate faster than others is class differences. Some ethnic and immigrant groups have higher education levels, job skills, and proficiency in English, giving them advantages in succeeding faster in their careers and having greater status in their society. As a result, they are able to achieve socioeconomic success faster than others can.

It really does not matter what method of assimilation you choose. What matters is that you make a genuine effort to learn, utilize, and practice American norms, traditions, habits, and social behaviors. By tuning into the new culture, the natives will know that you are willing to embrace the American way of doing things. They will pay more attention to you since familiarity breeds fondness and wins friendships.

The initial culture shock will be felt during your first three months in America. How badly you will be affected or not affected will depend upon how quickly you want to take positive steps to overcome the initial culture shock. Culture shock describes the anxiety produced when a person moves to a new environment. When you visit a new place, you are compelled to meet your everyday needs in new ways. No matter how much information you may have acquired beforehand, no matter how well you speak English, the initial culture shock will be stressful to some degree. You may have to eat different foods in a new manner or speak the language with a different accent. Yes, it can be stressful and be frustrating at times. However, it can be overcome with some positive learning processes in a short time.

The best way to overcome the initial culture shock is to not be judgmental. Keep all of your avenues open and have an open mind. If you are from a very conservative background, you may not like what is happening around you. However, you must pause and remember that there may be some positive elements to this new culture. Try to objectively analyze the differences that you are finding. How are they different from your habits and norms? There is always a good explanation for why Americans do things differently.

Make a gallant effort to try out a few new things. Do not worry about making mistakes. Americans usually understand. Their parents or grandparents were immigrants. They know very well what their ancestors had to go through when they first came to this country. Many of them have traveled all over the world and will know how to assist you in correcting your mistakes. You must, however, show that you are ready and willing to learn things and execute things according to American norms and traditions. If you make a mistake, laugh at yourself. Humor and a smile will take you places. However, avoid making any racial or sexist jokes.

I have adopted the cultural pluralism way of assimilation. I keep my traditional culture and Hindu religion intact, but I strive to share the common values, goals, traditions, social norms, and institutions that I like about American culture. I do not have to become highly Americanized and fear that I will be seen differently if I do not do things the American way. I am my own person. Your real identity comes from your family and your unique genetic code. So, be very proud of it. At the same time, take the best from the other cultures and traditions. By doing so, you can enjoy the very best that the two cultures have to offer.

Trust me—it is a foolproof approach to adapting to your new life in America.

CHAPTER 7:
AMERICAN CULTURE

When I first came to the United States, I had a preconceived notion that America did not have any real culture or traditions apart from uniquely American sports, Thanksgiving, a few national holidays, some pop culture, films, and music. I was under the impression that the United States was still a very young country and was still trying to emulate some of the British traditions and customs. I soon found out that I was quite wrong.

This wonderful country is indeed cultured. Its culture and traditions are embedded in its ideals, customs, beliefs, values, arts, and innovations. It includes elements that evolved from Europeans, Native Americans, and African Americans as well as different cultures from Latin America. It includes conservative and liberal factions, strong military, scientific, and political structures, and a hunger for free expression, along with materialistic and moral ideals. President Obama in his inaugural address was correct in stating that American society has been "shaped by every language and culture drawn from every end of the Earth" and that its citizens recognize that "our patchwork heritage is strength, not a weakness".

The harder and deeper I looked, the more things I found that are unique to American society and lifestyle. For example, people of this country devote lots of time and attention to American literature, cuisine, theater, TV, music, films, and fashion. Religion, architecture, and sculpture also play a major role in the hearts and minds of the American people.

Let's examine some of these topics and see how they contribute to the fabric of American society.

Religion

One of the prime elements that the federal constitution incorporates into the American dream is the freedom of religion. The founding fathers made it clear that the government should function according to the basic human decency and morale, not religion. A strict separation of church and government is declared in the American Constitution.

In 1787, the United States became one of the first countries in the world to codify religious freedom into its legal system. Among developed countries, America is one of the most religious in terms of its demographics. Religion plays a very important role in the lives of Americans. Followers of different religious faiths live side-by-side. Although Christians are in the majority (almost 75 percent), Jews, Buddhists, Hindus, Muslims, and even atheists are given their religious prominence and respect too. Churches, temples, ashrams, synagogues, and mosques are seen in every big city. Each religion has maintained it's unique theologies and traditions in America. This freedom of religion is an inalienable right and the government neither has any power of control nor can it prohibit the free exercise of anyone's religion no matter how outrageous someone's beliefs and practices are. This is an absolute right.

American Literature

American literature has also played a great role in enhancing American culture. By the middle of the nineteenth century, writers such as Nathaniel Hawthorne, Edgar Allan Poe, and David Thoreau had established a distinctive American literary style. America, by any standard, was producing outstanding literature by some brilliant authors.

How can one ignore authors such as Mark Twain, who is regarded as the greatest writer in American history? One should not forget the great American novels such as *Moby Dick,* by Herman Melville, *The Great Gatsby,* by F. Scott Fitzgerald, and *The Adventures of Huckleberry Finn,* by Mark Twain. These classics are studied in schools all over the world.

Sports

Sports are an important part of American culture. However, American preferences in sports differ from the rest of the world. For example, soccer is not nearly as popular in the United States as it is in many parts of the world.

Baseball is the oldest of the popular American sports. It was first started in 1869 and was a major sport for more than one hundred years before American football took center stage. Football is now the most popular sport in the nation. Its championship game, the Super Bowl, is the biggest sporting event in the country. Basketball is also gaining lots of fans. Professional basketball players are paid huge amounts of money. Ice hockey is also increasing in popularity and will, in time, have a much larger fan base.

Soccer, rugby, tennis, and golf are gaining new aficionados every year. These sports will probably never catch up with football, baseball, or basketball since they do not generate a high enough volume of ticket sales or capture the American imagination. These sports are also somewhat boring to watch for the majority of American audiences. Unless the media decides to encourage and foster these sports, American audiences will continue to spend their leisure time watching the three dominant sports.

Pop Culture

There is no denying that most pop culture has its roots in the United States. This country was the birthplace of global entertainment icons; Mickey Mouse, Bugs Bunny, Barbie, Elvis Presley, and Michael Jackson have all made unforgettable contributions to this culture. Almost everyone around the world—from kids to geriatrics—recognizes these popular American entertainers and appreciates their immense talent. I also grew up with this pop culture and enjoyed them all.

I always thought that Americans were innovative and creative; when I arrived in this country, my belief was confirmed. However, I did not realize how massive the entertainment business was until I visited Disneyland, Hollywood, and various movie studios in Los Angeles.

Music, Television, and Films

This country creates, produces, and releases many films, television shows, and popular songs every month. Entertainment is a huge industry, employing millions of people, and extraordinary amounts of money are spent producing movies and television shows. The entire world has enjoyed such movies as *Star Wars, The Godfather, Titanic, The Matrix,* and *Avatar.* Fans worldwide are familiar with such movie stars as George Clooney, Robert De Niro, Denzel Washington, Marlon Brando, and Brad Pitt.

The entertainment culture is not only appreciated by Americans, but also by the rest of the world. Its brilliance spills over international borders so that everyone can enjoy the extravagant productions.

I vividly recall when I first arrived in the United States, I asked a prominent local politician to explain to me few things about the American culture . He scratched his head for several minutes and stated "we really do not have much to boast about apart from Baseball, Apple Pie and Levi jeans but if I had to hedge my bet, it will be freedom, leadership, competition and entrepreneurship". I thought he gave a politically correct answer because at that time, I did not know much about my new adopted country. But now, having personally experienced the American lifestyle, I am glad I can add another five or six items to the list that he had not thought about. Some still argue that the British, the Europeans, the Russians , the Indians, the Chinese, the Japanese and dozen others handily beat the Americans in the cultural field but these are very old countries having evolved over thousands of years whereas America is a young country still in the throes of cultural revolution. It should never be forgotten that the United States and its people differ from other nations at least on historical basis since most of its citizens came from numerous places throughout the world with their own culture, customs and traditions. Thus, you will notice that American people prefer to talk about freedom, human rights, democracy, the rule of law, civil liberties fair play, private property etc., before bragging about their culture, customs and traditions.

Chapter 8:
Capitalism

"*America's abundance was not created by public sacrifices to the common good but by the productive genius of free men who pursued their own personal interests and the making of their own private fortunes. They did not starve the people to pay for America's industrialization. They gave the people better jobs, higher wages and cheaper goods with every new machine they invented, with every scientific discovery or technological advance—and thus the whole country was moving forward and profiting, not suffering, every step of the way.*"

—Ayn Rand

Everyone who comes to live in the United States—and those who are born here—knows the definition of words such as *democracy, freedom, civil rights, privacy rights, Americana, baseball,* and *apple pie.* However, there is another word that one should also be familiar with: *capitalism.* One will invariably hear this word almost every day. It has become part of the fabric of American society. The citizens of this nation can't even imagine life under any other kind of economic system. It's as though the idea has taken on a sacred significance in the collective consciousness of the people.

45

Unless you have minimal knowledge of this economic system and how it works, you cannot call yourself a true American. Americans are very aware of their rights, responsibilities, and civic duties. They know that their country is an economic superpower and understand the ideology of free markets. If you work hard, save money, and make the right investments, you can become a millionaire. This country is full of rags-to-riches stories. That is why everything is possible in America and is the main reason why millions want to live in this country.

Capitalism can be explained as an economic and social system in which individuals privately control their hard-earned money. With the money that they earn, they can hire labor or services and turn their ingenuity and ideas into profits. Goods and services are exchanged for money or property. Furthermore, it is also a system based on individual rights. Capitalism recognizes that each and every person is the owner of his or her own life. Each person has the right to live and work in the manner he or she chooses—as long as it does not violate the rights of others. In a communist system, the property is controlled by the central government. The government controls every single piece of capital. There are no classes of people; no one is wealthy and no one is poor. That is the theory; in the real world, it is not quite true. A very small ruling class always owns most of the wealth.

In capitalism, one of the important principles is the role of the government in protecting and safeguarding individual rights. This is achieved by an efficient police force, a powerful military to protect from foreign aggression, and a good judicial system to settle disputes between citizens. These are some of the principles that the founding fathers envisioned—and America has embraced.

Is capitalism a fair and just social system? The answer is a big yes because all individuals are considered equal under the laws of the United States. Capitalism recognizes that it is just and fair for a man to keep what he has earned. In my opinion, all other economic systems, such as communism and socialism, do the citizen an injustice by legally expropriating the property of one group of hardworking people and distributing it to others. One may strongly argue that capitalism is not a fair and just system, especially when you see that famous athletes making a hundred times more than a highly recognized rocket scientist with a PhD who works much longer and strenuous hours. Yet, when you really think about it, this situation is quite fair. An athlete creates enormous profits though ticket sales and endorsements. The scientist generates very little revenue in comparison. Since each man has the right to the product of his labor, it is completely just for the disparity of incomes to exist between a professional athlete and a rocket scientist.

The other point is that democracy rests on the principle of individual rights. Capitalism is, in a way, directly related to democracy, especially the type of democracy that is inherent in the US Constitution. Under the American system of democracy, the powers of judges and policemen are strictly defined, limiting their actions and powers. In communist and socialist societies, these powers of the government are very broad and the human rights of the people are often trampled or abused, causing ordinary citizens to suffer. Their governments have unbridled powers capable of doing anything—even to the extent of taking your house and wealth without reason.

The competition among capitalists promotes the growth of individuals. This makes working life easier. It creates motivation, giving a person the will, drive, and determination to work harder. Government regulations help by preventing corporations from committing fraud or using deceptive practices. The best thing in the capitalist system is that any ordinary worker—by working hard, being frugal, and with a little bit of luck and proper investments—can become a business owner. He can provide his goods and services and make profits. With profits, he can grow and flourish. In this country, a lot depends on how hard a person is willing to work in order to become wealthy. It gives its citizens the opportunity to go out and make as much money as possible— as long as it is earned legitimately.

Granted, it is not going to be easy. Sometimes people work really hard and save every penny, but cannot elevate themselves from the ranks of the poor. It may be due to the lack of proper investment, insufficient monetary knowledge, poor health, large family responsibilities, or dozens of other reasons. Nevertheless, under the capitalist system, the opportunity is always there. The government with its laws and regulations is supportive of its citizens to go out and find ways and means to become rich.

The government intervention in the private ownership makes the American style of capitalist system even more beneficial for everyone. This is because Americans do believe that some services are more efficiently performed by the government agencies. For instance, in the United States, the government is responsible for administration of justice, education, road systems, unemployment benefits and few others. Whenever it has to, the government also steps in to regulate and break up large corporate monopolies. The government uses anti-trust laws to control the corporate attempt to monopolize in certain areas of commerce. This is done to control prices, for product safety and for health and welfare of its citizens. Consequently, one may argue that Americans have made a shift from pure form of capitalism towards mixed economy in certain respects. This would be a fair assessment.

You cannot go wrong by choosing to live under the American style of capitalist system. "America is the Canaan of capitalism, here the tendencies of Western capitalism could find its fullest and most uncontrolled expression," wrote a German economist , Werner Sombart in 1906. Another author and economist

William N. Parker in his book " A Short History of American Capitalism" commented "It was the Americans who created the phrase 'to make money.' No other language or nation had ever used these words before; men had always thought of wealth as a static quantity—to be seized, begged, inherited, shared, looted, or obtained as a favor. Americans were first to understand that wealth was to be created."

CHAPTER 9:
SHOPPING CRAZY NATION

A quote in *Mad Magazine* has been stuck in my mind forever. It was something like this. "The only reason an American family does not own an elephant is that the pet stores have never offered an elephant for a dollar down with easy monthly payments." This was meant to be a joke, but how true it is. Americans will buy anything—from pet rocks to an elephant—just to satisfy their insatiable appetite for possessions.

In most parts of the world, people only go to stores and markets because they have to, in order to purchase the necessities of life. However, for millions of Americans, shopping has evolved into a recreational activity. They do it because they want to—not because they have to. This incredible zest for consumer goods is one of the reasons why the American economy has been leading the world for decades. We now import more products than we manufacture, which only goes to prove that, if you make it, Americans will buy it.

Indeed, one of the favorite pastimes in this country is shopping. Some people see this as an ordinary pleasure, others see it as habit, and some admit that they have a shopping addiction. Shopping for clothes, shoes, food, books, DVDs, CDs, electronic goods, furniture, cars, and appliances—the list goes on. Americans shop till they drop or shop till they rock—especially during Christmas season. One will seldom find any shopping mall empty on any given day. Most of the shops remain open until nine o'clock at night. The retail shops, restaurants, and fast-food places all get their fair share of business. Americans love shopping and there really is no need for any incentive to entice them to the stores and malls. TV commercials, billboard advertising, coupons, pressure from peers, and children's demands—as well as necessities—are some of the reasons that consumers constantly buy sometimes-unneeded stuff.

The credit card and impulse to use it without a second thought and the easy availability of credit from large department stores exacerbates the problem of overspending. One has to be careful with credit cards. Some reports indicate that people who use credit cards tend to spend 20–30 percent more than they would if they had to pay by cash. Internet shopping is also being touted in a big way in this country. You have to be careful while browsing for merchandise on the Internet. Just one click of a mouse can put a few more dollars of debt on your credit card. My economics professor once said, "Credit buying is much like being drunk. The buzz happens immediately and gives you a lift, but the hangover comes few days after." How true!

Whatever the reasons, the addiction to shopping is so bad that the term "shopaholic" has been coined to apply to those who are always shopping whether or not they need any stuff. Children love to shop, the elderly love to shop, and middle-aged parents—especially women—have to shop for themselves, their families, pets, relatives, and friends. Buying gifts, groceries, clothes, home decorations, and spending for house repairs is the norm. People often miss work in order to go shopping. The habit of constantly buying stuff is the reason that most American homes are cluttered with furniture, closets full of clothes, pantries full of food, and family rooms full of gadgets and equipment. For some people, the addiction to shopping is so severe that they have to seek professional counseling or therapy to assist them in quitting this habit. Across the country, there are psychiatrists who regularly see and treat compulsive shoppers. Prescription drugs sometimes have to be dispensed to curtail this habit.

Many in this country have no savings and no money for the rainy days because they spend their extra money on unnecessary stuff. A lot of these items, especially clothes, are discarded after a couple of uses. The garage is usually the dumping place, but so are closets, attics, spare rooms, or underneath beds—anyplace where there is room to store things. This is one of the reasons why you will see many storage buildings all over the country. They do a roaring business. People do not have enough space in their homes for all the things they keep on buying. This is what some call crazy consumerism. Some even call it an addiction equivalent to gambling. The lesson is to keep your buying habits under control and watch where your dollars are spent.

To balance this picture, it must not to be forgotten that this sort of high-volume consumerism is what keeps the American economy robust and allows money to stay in circulation. It provides jobs for millions, it keeps small businesses' cash registers humming, and allows sales and business taxes to be collected by the government. That is the reason why American presidents sometimes encourage their citizens to keep on spending. President Bush did it in the wake of the 9/11 crisis and President Obama did it recently by encouraging the "Cash for Clunkers" federal spending program to entice people into buying new cars that are more fuel efficient to help prop up slumping auto sales. The so called "black Friday" is the day after Thanksgiving when millions of Americans go shopping. Some department stores open as early as four o' clock in the morning and throngs of shoppers wait in line for the front door of stores to open. Some even camp overnight to get in the store first and take advantage of highly publicized major discounts. This helps the economy in a big way and some store owners wish that there were another half a dozen black Fridays because it helps boost their profit margins.

Everyone should know a few things about their rights as consumers. If there is something wrong with the merchandise or the service provided or you have to return the merchandize, then every so often, you will have to assert your rights. Essentially, there are six basic consumer rights.

- The Right to be Safe: This right implies that any product that has been purchased should cause no harm to their users if such an item is properly used as prescribed. The Consumer Product Safety Commission has jurisdiction. They often ask for a product recall when they think that a product is defective or will cause harm or injuries to buyers. The recall of vehicles is one such example.
- The Right to Choose Freely: This right states that consumers should have a variety of options provided by different companies from which to choose. This right tries to prevent monopolistic business practices and price gouging. It also encourages competition. Competition brings down prices of goods and services. Thus, the consumer benefits.
- The Right to be Heard: This right gives consumers the ability to voice their complaints and concerns about a product. The state and federal attorney generals have the powers to deal with this sort of complaint. In addition, the Better Business Bureau is a national non-governmental entity that provides

help to consumers by providing background information about many businesses within their district. They keep a record of complaints, licenses, bonds, insurance information, and the age of the company. They are very helpful on the phone.

- The Right to be Informed: This right states that businesses should always provide consumers with enough appropriate, honest information to make sound and informed choices about the product that they intend to buy. It requires that product information should always be complete and truthful.

- The Right to Education: This right to provide consumers access to programs and information helps them to make better marketplace decisions.

- The Right to Service: This right ensures consumers that they shall be treated with courtesy and respect, that businesses will be responsive to their customers' needs and problems, and that everyone should have the right to refuse any services offered.

From time to time, you may have problems with your phone, electric, water, or garbage companies. You should first try to speak with the management, but if the problem still has not been resolved, then you must contact the Public Utilities Commission. Once a complaint is filed with the commission, they will investigate and provide a resolution or direct you to the right place for further investigation.

Furthermore, one must always be aware that there are scam artists operating all over the country. They will try to sell you get rich quick schemes and/or snake oil. They will be all over you and will intentionally make fraudulent and misleading statements. If you are not careful, you will get duped out of your money. If it sounds too good to be true, then it is—stay away from it! Any transactions with these scammers are designed to rip you off. Be extra careful when approached by suspicious vendors. They will be ruthless and tell you blatant lies to get your money. The Federal Trade Commission publishes a guide describing common frauds and fraudulent schemes. If in doubt, go online and check things out or ask around. Someone will know about it.

Furthermore, you should also know about warranty laws stating that the product being sold would meet or exceed its intended purpose. The notion of implied warranty places the onus on the seller to not to sell defective products. But, there will always be unscrupulous sellers who will try to defraud you. Most warranty laws give consumers three days time to opt out if they change their minds and decide not to purchase the merchandise.

The Truth in Lending Act requires complete disclosure of any costs and interest rates pertaining to loans paid on installment. This has been enacted to prevent lenders from charging any hidden costs. There are also laws directed at labeling and packaging. These laws require accurate content descriptions and the identification of all applicable dangers associated with the product. A good example is the Cigarette Labeling Act of 1965. It gives health warnings inherent in smoking.

The meaning of the words "buyer be aware" should also be learnt. It essentially means that a buyer of a product must examine, analyze, ponder, judge and test a product before paying for it. Once you buy it then you will most likely be stuck with it no matter how defective or useless the product is. This is mostly true when buying something on "as is" basis, like automobiles, boats, used appliances etc.

The bottom line is to know your rights. If large, expensive items are involved, such as cars or a house, resist pressure to make your decision right away. Ask a friend or a family member for advice. Sometimes, you may want to consult your accountant or lawyer for advice. Do not let embarrassment or fear prevent you from seeking good advice. Do not forget to read the fine print and make sure that you understand the terms and conditions of the loans and other financial documents.

Chapter 10:
A Good Credit History

How is your credit? Do you know your credit score? If not, you probably should, because the modern American economy is based in large part on your credit rating. It's nearly impossible to live the good life without strong credit. Working hard and doing your best is no longer good enough in the modern era. In order to truly enjoy all of the luxuries in America, such as a good house, a nice car, top-notch furnishings, and appliances, then you need to make sure that your credit is in good standing. Without good credit, no bank or financial institution will ever give you a loan. The entire country runs on borrowed money from big banks, credit unions, and financial institutions. Everyone, even if they have ample cash sitting in the bank, gets loans to buy a house or a car, to have the house remodeled, to start a business, or to send their kids to college.

Many employers will want to check your credit history before hiring you. They just want to see if the person that they are about to hire is a responsible, ethical, and trustworthy person. As jobs become more competitive, more employers are doing credit checks. If you are seeking a position in accounting, finance, or banking, then you can bet your last dollar that a credit check will have to be done with your permission before any decision is made. One report indicates that 60 percent of employers will want to check a prospective employee's credit history. You will be entitled to see the copy of your report if a decision not to give you the job is based on your credit report. It is of utmost importance in this country to have a good credit history.

In order to get a loan, the first thing any lending institution will want to check is your credit history. If your credit history is not in good standing, then no matter how many co-signers you have, how much you plead, or how much collateral you present, they will not want to have any sort of loan dealings with you. Without loans, it will be very difficult to have and enjoy the luxuries in life that we all want. In this country, when a customer fills out an application for a secured loan from bank, their information is sent to a credit bureau. There are three credit-reporting agencies in America (Experian, Equifax, and Trans Union). The credit bureau will then match the applicant's name and identifying information with the information that these bureaus keep. This information tells the bank whether you are creditworthy. Creditworthiness means whether an individual is capable of repaying his debt. The issue of control of debt is also very important to lenders. Lenders want to see that applicants are not living beyond their means. The lenders are interested in seeing how stable the applicant is. Thus, having a longstanding job, some savings, and some risk factors, such as having bought small items on credit from department stores, should be tried first. Lenders are interested in seeing whether the applicant pays his obligations on time and how solid his financial strength is. A good credit reputation is of utmost importance in this country. Some of the factors revealed in the credit report help lenders to determine whether to extend credit and on what terms. The report is also very important to determine the interest rates, grace period, and term of the loan. But, be careful -these reports are sometimes erroneous. The applicant can dispute it and fast results of the dispute are provided by the credit bureaus as provided by the consumer laws.

Your credit history is very important to get a credit card. Without a few credit cards, you simply cannot operate in American society. It is like a consumer passport since lots of places do not even take cash for their merchandise. Checks are going out of fashion and cash transactions are seen as risky, cumbersome, and somewhat antiquated. Merchants, vendors, and storekeepers feel vulnerable when large amounts of cash are handed to them. They think about gangs, the Mafia, counterfeits, and drug money and are reluctant to make cash deals. Many people do not want to carry cash with them in case they are mugged or robbed.

Having a solid credit history and possessing at least two credit cards is of utmost importance in order to make any kind of material progress. The buying power of any person in this country depends on his credit history. If your credit history is bad, you will not be able to purchase anything of value. Things such as bankruptcy, foreclosure, and repossessions put a major dent in your credit history and ought to be avoided as much as possible.

A good credit score will be in the range of 650 to 725—and 800 is seen as excellent. If you are in this range, then every bank and other financial institutions will want to give you a loan if you qualify. A person's credit score is based on 35 percent payment history and 30 percent debt-to-credit ratio; the rest is based on length of credit history, type of credit account, and other factors.

Credit History of Immigrants: Credit history usually applies to only one country. Different countries do not share information. For example, if a person has been living in Canada for many years and then moves to the United States and applies for a loan, he will not be approved because of lack of credit history—even if they had an excellent credit history in Canada. An immigrant must establish a good credit history in this country from scratch. Therefore, it is very hard for immigrants to obtain credit cards and mortgages until after they have worked in this country with a reasonably good income for at least two years.

Ways to secure a good credit history include:

- Paying your bills on time. Good financial management starts with punctuality. Formulate a sensible budget plan and stick to it.
- Learning how to save money for bad times. If you start saving 5 percent of your wages every month, it will amount to something. This will see you through tough times, such as a job loss, serious illness, or emergency travel to your home country. Practice self-restraint. Just because you want something desperately does not mean you need to have it as soon as possible. Your immediate needs of food, shelter, clothing, rent, and utilities must be given priority. If there is a little bit left over, then you can spend that to purchase things that you really desire.
- Avoid seeking and applying for loans for a while. Try to pay your financial obligations with your own means. Budgeting and planning in advance should give you this ability to pay as you go.
- Avoid opening more credit lines than you need. Every line of credit results in a ten-point deduction in your credit score. Some department stores will sometimes urge you to apply for credit. They also charge exorbitant interest rates. Seeing interest rates as much as 28 percent should not surprise you. Think twice before opening a credit line.

Maintaining a good credit history requires a great deal of discipline. One has to act financially responsible. No matter how wealthy one gets, there is an absolute need for good financial planning. You can check your credit report every now and then and find out your scores. Free credit reports can be obtained from reporting agencies once a year. You need to know your credit score so that you will not be misled by lenders or reporting agencies. Reporting agencies sometimes make mistakes. It happens from time to time when a person's name and address is mixed up with someone with a similar name. It can be difficult to clear that confusion. Always remember that the interest rates that you will be offered will be affected by your credit history. The higher the credit rating, the lower the interest rates. Seek lower interest rates if you know you have good credit reputation and have a high score. Also be aware that, in the United States, a lender is required by law to tell applicants why a loan was denied. The lender must also provide the name and address of the credit-reporting agency that provided data that was used to make the denial decision. You will have to find out from the agency in detail what your report entails and determine whether it is accurate.

The credit reporting agencies will not decide whether an applicant's credit history is unworthy- it is the lender that makes the decision. Since each lender has its own policies and guidelines, it is possible that a lender will make a favorable decision even though a person's credit history is not all that great. Sometimes, your loan officer can do you great favors.

CHAPTER 11:
HEALTH ISSUES AND MEDICAL BENEFITS

No matter where you live, it's impossible to enjoy life without good health. While some of that may come down to genes, lifestyle, or even just luck, the quality of health care makes a big difference. Modern medical facilities staffed by highly trained professionals can help people live longer, healthier lives. Nobody has better—or more available—health care than the United States of America.

Think for a moment about why this is so important. Whenever we embark on a new venture or undertaking or have important adventures to pursue, we do not want any interruptions, confrontations, crises, or catastrophes in our lives. The focus should always be on the ultimate goal and that is to find legitimate ways and means of becoming prosperous and successful.

We were also of the same mindset when we first arrived in this country. We wanted to live without problems or tension. Our main objective was to get settled in our new country and try to learn the ropes of daily living as fast as we could. However, there came a time when we found out that my wife was pregnant. We were thrilled. We had wanted to have another child for quite some time and family members were teasing us for being too afraid to expand our family. My wife's pregnancy went very well with no major incidents. She had a good doctor who examined her every three months—and every time, the examination results turned out to be just great.

Then came the delivery day. On a cold December morning, I had to take my wife to the hospital. My parents came to our house and babysat our daughter, Suhani, while I took my wife to the hospital. After enduring a few hours of labor, my wife gave birth to a beautiful eight pound, six ounce girl. After our initial exhilaration and rejoicing, we came to accept that we now had two beautiful daughters. The nurses and doctors briefly examined our baby. She was bathed and cleaned and the doctors started to take a serious look at her again. Some five hours later, the doctor came into my wife's hospital room and wanted to speak to us. At that time, we had no clue what he wanted to share. I thought my new baby had some complication, such as jaundice, or maybe some sort of physical disability, such as an extra finger.

The doctor, a well-known pediatrician, started his opening remarks by talking about genes and chromosomes and making sure that we understood some of the medical terminology and its meanings. He discussed having children with disabilities and the chances of their survival. He very gently broke the news that our daughter had Down's syndrome. She would need all sorts of special help and would look different from us; she would also have physical and mental challenges.

We had seen a few other Down's babies and were somewhat familiar with what they looked like and how they behaved. Still, we found it very hard to process the thought that we were going to be parents of a handicapped child. We were numb and dumbfounded for several minutes. We then started to ask questions, such as, whether she would be able to dress herself, speak, feed and clean herself, and attend school. We were not quite sure how to react. Tears of sorrow rolled from our eyes and our hearts sank. Our minds were gushing with thoughts about any cures that might be found anywhere in this world, any prayers that we could say that would cure our daughter, and any religious rites or rituals that we could perform that may get our daughter cured. The answers were all negative. We were lost. We were told that counseling for handling children with Down's syndrome was readily available and all we had to do was to seek that help. In the meantime, our little girl was sleeping after getting her first bath and a thorough medical checkup. We looked at her beautiful face and lovely body and were in total disbelief that she would grow up to be a developmentally challenged child. We named her Cahani, meaning a "beautiful story," which she is. She has a story in her mind and a story in her life to reveal. She is also the story of our lives.

For the next several months, we received professional help from Down's syndrome groups, special nurses, and counseling from specialized, highly trained counselors. There were different types of blood testing, a weekly examination, and initial fine motor therapy for Cahani. Several books and tapes were made available to us, several doctors gave us advice, and everyone tried to console us by telling us that things would be all right and that Cahani would have a lifetime of assistance from the state. Had Cahani been born in some other country, I do not think we would have received one-quarter of the professional help and medical assistance that we have received in this country.

If American doctors and medical science technicians and equipment cannot treat your ailments, disease, or sickness, then nowhere in the world would you be able to receive any better medical assistance. This is the country in which one should be living if one has some major health problems. The hospitals, doctors, and nurses of this country are highly trained and deliver excellent service. You need good medical insurance, and the premiums that you pay are worthwhile when you face a major medical crisis.

As time went by, counseling and education made some sense to us, explaining why God had given us this angelic daughter. We gradually started to accept the fact that we would have to take one day at a time and make this beautiful girl's life wonderful and fill it with joy and happiness. We were thoroughly thankful that she was born in the United States since we had all the social support, medical assistance, and modern technology at our disposal to help her achieve her full potential. We were grateful that we were surrounded by professionals in the medical and social behavior fields who were ready and willing to help. We were thoroughly delighted that we were living in the most progressive and medically advanced country in the world. Above all, we were assured that Cahani would be treated the same as any other American citizen.

After some therapy to develop her fine motor skills and heart surgery to close some holes in her heart, Cahani went to school and completed high school. Although she mainly attended the special education classes, she developed good social skills and her mental abilities have advanced to quite a high level. Cahani still attends special education classes since she will not be able to hold a job, but she eats, cleans, and dresses on her own. Her fine motor skills have developed very well to the extent that she can extract fish bones from a fish while eating. She loves and thoroughly enjoys dancing, singing, and swimming. She is an avid Bollywood movie fan and watches several Hindi movies every month and remembers most of the dance numbers and songs from each movie. She loves to travel and enjoys staying in beautiful, expensive hotels. Under Americans For Disabilities Act of 1990, any sort of discrimination against people with disabilities is strictly prohibited. It is a comprehensive anti-discrimination law that extends to virtually all areas of society and to every aspect of daily living of disabled people. One should not hesitate to use the provisions of this Act if your beloved one has been discriminated in getting a job, accommodation, transportation, social services and so forth. Go to website www.ada.gov for more information.

Health Benefits

This brings me to a brief discussion about the current health-care system in the United States. With the advent of the Health Care Reform Act of 2010 passed by the Obama administration, there are going to be major changes. However, the full effect of these changes will not be implemented until 2014. The most important thing to keep in mind for the present is that, in the United States, the operation of the health-care system is mainly in the hands of private health-care corporations. There is no national system of government-owned medical facilities for the general public. We do not have a socialized medical system in this country such as in the United Kingdom or Canada. In some locations, states or counties own and operate hospitals, but they are few and scattered all over in different parts of the states. There are also federal hospitals, but they only serve veterans and active military personnel and their families.

About 60 percent of Americans receive their health insurance coverage through their employer. The employer and the employee share the premium and some employees with families can pay up to 28 percent of their gross pay for health insurance. In addition, most employees have to pay deductibles and co-payments. Health insurance can take a big chunk of your paycheck. The medications that are prescribed by the doctors have to be purchased from local pharmacies and a certain co-payment has to be paid to the pharmacist before the medicine is dispensed. This can also become an expensive commodity, depending on the type and brand of medicine.

If you do not have a job, you can purchase individual health insurance, but it that can cost as much as $350 per month for a family of four. Most employers with more than fifty employees provide some medical benefits. Most of the unemployed and new immigrants go without any health insurance. Some data has shown that approximately 38 million people in this country do not have any type of health insurance. This is a major problem and has generated a great deal of debate. The Obama administration is trying to find a reasonable solution. The Health Care Reform laws will enable every American to obtain some sort of health insurance by 2014. Few main features of the new legislation will be that you will be able to buy insurance directly in an Exchange if your employer does not offer health insurance. The Exchange will offer a choice of health plans that can be purchased rather cheaply. And, if an affordable coverage is not available than you can be eligible for an exemption. The other thing that will help the poor is that if you earn less than one hundred and thirty three percent of the poverty level then you will be entitled to be enrolled in medic-aid system. There are some other very beneficial provisions in the new legislation that should be carefully studied and noted.

What is a newly arrived immigrant with no job supposed to do if he or his family member becomes seriously injured or becomes very ill requiring immediate medical attention? The answer for the time being will be that he or she should go to the nearest hospital's emergency department. In 1986, the federal government enacted the "Emergency Medical Treatment and Active Labor Act," requiring hospital emergency departments to treat emergency conditions for all patients—regardless of their ability to pay. Thus, an emergency department cannot just turn you away. They have to give you proper medical care and then get compensated through state and federal reimbursement programs. Emergency departments do not provide any non-emergency treatments or any type of preventive care. Moreover, one will find that the emergency department is always filled to capacity. That means long waits can be anticipated—especially in urban hospitals. The patients are prioritized according to the seriousness of their conditions.

Sometimes these hospitals will attempt to bill the uninsured patient directly under the fee-for-service program. This is done when state and federal programs, for some less obvious reasons, fail to compensate. Thus, if you get a bill from the hospital, it should not be ignored. Call them or write to them and tell the hospital administrators you don't have a job, and have no money or other assets. The hospital will know that the patient cannot afford to pay and will not give it to a collection agency. Once it gets to the collection agency, the collectors will hound you with phone calls and letters. It is better to resolve it with the hospital's billing department amicably. The ambulance bill will also be tendered for payment if the patient had to be transported by ambulance. If you can prove that you have no income or assets, there is nothing to worry about. The hospital will often write it off as bad debt.

Whatever the circumstances, the thing to remember is that if you get sick or injured in the United States, you will get world-class treatment. However, do not forget that the person who got treatment will receive a hefty bill that can sometimes defy any logic. One night's hospital stay can cost as much as $3,500 plus the ambulance bill, which can also add up to hundreds of dollars, depending on distance and care. Many people have filed for personal bankruptcy because they were unable to pay off medical debts. One study found that 62 percent of persons declaring bankruptcy in 2007 had listed unpaid medical expenses of over five thousand dollars. If you own property and have a job, a medical lien can easily be imposed on your wages and possessions.

In view of the above, it would be a good idea to have your general health, dental, and vision care needs be taken care of before you leave your homeland. It would also be wise to get your doctor to prescribe you at least three months of any necessary medications. If you get your prescriptions filled before you leave your country, you will not have to worry about your medications or the costs associated with it for three months.

CHAPTER 12:
NEED HELP? SEEK AND YOU SHALL FIND

Nobody can really ever know in advance what life is going to hand them. Even hardworking, honest people sometimes get knocked down by circumstances beyond their control. America may be the richest nation on earth, but it has always had its share of folks who struggle to make ends meet. They are barely able to feed themselves and their families—and may not even be able to keep a roof over their heads. Fortunately, America has built an elaborate public and private network of assistance for those in need.

America's state, federal, and local municipal agencies, and various private charitable organizations and citizens are ready, willing, and able to assist anyone with basic needs. It does not matter if you need food, clothing, medical care, shelter, or just a small amount of cash. Someone will help you, but you must know how to go about seeking this type of help. You must know where to turn in times of desperation. You will find that the first three years in this country will probably be the toughest for you. You are adjusting to changes and trying to slowly feel your way around. Your career is probably insecure and you are still trying to learn some of the bureaucratic systems and, of course, learning and educating yourself as you go along. A time may come when you may lose your job, your apartment, have no savings, and have no one to turn to for assistance. Your family members are probably in the same boat and your few friends are also trying to keep afloat. You do not want to become homeless and do not want to become a burden on anyone that is close to you. You may be desperate for help. If you get sick, desperation may lead to related physical, mental, and financial problems. This is the time for you to seek help from the network of federal, state, and local government and local volunteer agencies.

The first thing you need to do is to get on the Internet and go to www.GovBenefits.gov. This is a great place to start your inquiries to see if you are eligible for any type of assistance. It is available in English and Spanish and was started by the Department of Labor. Sixteen federal agencies are participants of this program. You will have to complete an online questionnaire and the site will match you with programs most suited to your needs. It may take some time to get a response from one of the agencies, but your application will be reviewed and you will be contacted. This is a good start.

If you are really desperate, unemployed, hungry, and broke, then you need to know about the food stamp program that is operated by Department of Agriculture. The government distributes millions of dollars of food stamps to millions of people every year. The application for food stamps can be made at any Social Security office. Usually a family of four with monthly gross income of $2,238 per month or less qualifies. There are many other restrictions and one of them is that you must register for work. You may first want to check www.foodstamps-step.1.usda.gov to see if you qualify and what the eligibility requirements are. Your children may be eligible for the free or reduced school breakfast and lunch. The school guidance counselor or principal should be your first contacts. Food banks are another source for nutritious food for almost free. One can obtain a list of these programs from the local county-operated social welfare department.

Medi-Cal is a very important program (in California) for immigrants to resort to if they become seriously ill and are still unemployed and uninsured. You need to understand that there is a significant difference between the Medicare and Medi-Cal programs. Medi-Cal is a state health-care program for certain individuals and families who are low income and have limited resources.

Medi-Cal beneficiaries are issued a beneficiary identification card. It is meant to be used by low-income people, seniors, disabled persons, and poor citizens who have a serious diseases, such as cancer, tuberculosis, or AIDS. You have to qualify for this program and the qualifications are quite stringent. All immigrants must show documentation of satisfactory immigration status. The state must verify the information provided in a non-discriminatory manner. To apply for Medi-Cal, contact your local county social services office. There are similar programs in other states.

On the other hand, the **Medicare** program is a federal health insurance program for people sixty-five or older. Most people get Medicare because they are eligible for Social Security retirement or disability insurance benefits. This program is administered by the Centers for Medicare and Medicaid Services. You can get more information about Medicare from your local Social Security office.

Emergency medical treatment in the emergency department is a federally operated program. As mentioned before, if you or a member of your family gets very sick or seriously hurt, then you must seek medical assistance in any hospital's emergency room. Once you go to the emergency department, the hospital will have to examine you and determine whether you need immediate treatment. The hospital cannot turn you away. The patient will have to be stabilized, treated, and then released. The hospital may not delay an examination or treatment because the patient does not have health insurance or some method of payment. There can be no retaliation against a physician or hospital staff member who registered the patient. Furthermore, hospitals must post a sign in emergency rooms regarding the policy on patients' rights and, if these rights are violated, a fine up to $50,000 can be imposed on the hospital.

There are also health-care centers created under the federal law. These are called "FQHC" enters. These clinics provide basic health-care services to low-income, uninsured residents, including dental screening, family planning, immunization services, and assistance to get into the Medi-Cal system. These health-care centers are widely used in rural areas.

Most counties have at least one hospital that sees patients who are uninsured if it is their last resort. However, the degree to which a particular county provides services that are not covered by Medi-Cal or other programs varies from county to county.

Healthy Families for Children is a program for children under the age of eighteen, providing free medical and dental treatment. Parents have to qualify their children for this program. Children who are in some way disabled enough to keep them from doing well in school or to go to work may qualify for Social Security benefits. They will get monthly benefits.

In addition, one must not forget getting help from church groups, charitable organizations, private companies, the Red Cross, Salvation Army, and even some doctors who provide free medical advice and treatment. These organizations do not require you to prove your identity or resident status.

The idea and motive should not be to become dependent upon public benefits and subsistence. You should use these services only as a last resort and make use of them sparingly. You have to be careful not to become a public charge—an immigrant who is likely to become primarily dependent on the government for subsistence. The government will look at the records to see how much public cash assistance for income maintenance you have received. You have to be careful. Some people have been deported for becoming a public charge. Also, your sponsor who filed the affidavit on your behalf may be compelled to reimburse the government for all monetary assistance provided. This will undoubtedly create more stress and tension amongst your friends and family members.

The other thing to keep in mind is that prescription drugs can be very expensive. Try to get generic drugs that are much cheaper than the original medicine. Big retail stores, such as Walmart, Costco, and Target pharmacies, are usually cheaper than other places. Sometimes you can contact the drug manufacturer and some of them will have prescription assistance programs. They will provide medicines at cheaper prices.

Ask your doctor if they have any samples of medicines prescribed. They will be happy to provide you with a couple of days prescribed dose. These free samples will save you a few dollars.

Housing assistance is a very important issue to know about since it affects the biggest expenditure that you will have and it takes a large chunk of your income. Housing is very expensive in the United States and you have to be careful where you rent, who you rent from, and the terms and conditions of the rental. Some landlords are unscrupulous and will try to rent you apartments in deplorable condition at prime rental value. Others will try to rent you an apartment that has all types of problems, such as very old paint, poor plumbing, dirty carpets, or a leaky roof at high prices and will take a two-month security deposit and one month's cleaning deposit. You have to be careful while inspecting the apartment, signing the lease, and paying money up front.

If times get tough and you have a low income and two or more children, you may want to look into public housing. Section 8 housing is administered by the Department of Housing and Urban Development (HUD). Although it is a federal program, it is administered by local public housing agencies (PHAs). PHAs receive federal funds from HUD to administer a voucher program. You have to contact the local PHA office to apply for this subsidy. Apart from this program, PHA may be administering other public housing programs. It would be worthwhile to ask about other housing programs as well. The demand for housing assistance is usually very high and long waiting periods are common.

Under Section 8, eligible participants are free to choose any housing that meets the requirement of the program, but it is limited to units in subsidized housing projects. Once the house is rented, the family that is issued a voucher is responsible for finding suitable housing. Rental units must meet minimum standards of health and safety. The housing subsidy is paid to the landlord directly by the PHA. The family pays the difference between the actual rent and the amount being subsidized. The rent has to be very reasonable, taking into account the size, location, and overall condition of the dwelling.

The tenant, landlord, HUD, and PHA all have a certain responsibilities under the voucher program. PHA must inspect the dwelling every six months and make sure that the place is safe and secure and that the rent charged is reasonable. The tenant's obligation is to sign the lease and pay the rent. The lease is usually signed for one year. When the family is settled in the new home, they are expected to comply with the terms of the lease, pay their share of the rent, maintain the unit in good condition, and notify PHA if there is any change in income status or if the landlord is being too intrusive. PHA will have to be advised if there is any change in income, addition to the family, or any habitability problems.

There is assistance available for low-income families in using public transport, whether it is traveling by train, bus, ferry, taxi, or other mode of transportation. The best place to start is to ask your local public transportation agency. They will ask you to fill out an extensive application. The agency will then have it reviewed by the transportation authority. Often they will deny it, but if they approve it, then you will get a pass and the transportation agency will pay up to 80 percent of the fare. The cost to the passenger could be as low as fifty cents per ride. For disabled people and senior citizens, there are non-profit organizations, such as Para Transit Inc., whose main role is to provide transportation services to individuals who are disabled or elderly and unable to drive.

There are other programs that provide services to passengers to conduct their day-to-day activities, such as doctor's appointments, school, shopping, or errands.

General public assistance is readily and widely provided to low-income citizens. The catch is that you have to be eligible for each program. Different agencies have different requirements. The application process may take some time and, depending on the program, sometimes the wait can be as long as six months. Each city, county, and state has its own program. It is a matter of finding out about these programs. There is no reason to be ashamed in accepting these programs—as long as you know that you and your family are genuinely trying to get on your feet. Your application must be made with utmost honesty, in good faith, and with sincerity and integrity. The objective of these programs is to get a person some help while he or she is trying to find employment and seeking some sort of stability in life. If you have young children, then your chances of getting into these programs will be somewhat enhanced. Public assistance is for those who are genuinely eligible for it and require it as a necessity. This country looks after its poor, hungry, homeless, disabled, and downtrodden. The United States is generous and compassionate, but it is not a welfare country. However, it is very sensitive to the needs of its poor citizens.

CHAPTER 13:
THE LEGAL SYSTEM

When I first arrived in this country, one of the scariest things for me was seeing some of the security guards and all of the police officers carrying guns. I was simply not used to that because in my homeland and in other countries that I had visited, police officers were not armed with guns. They carried batons and relied on their physical and intellectual powers and muscles. Therefore, it was a very strange sight for me and it took some time to overcome that kind of visual. I also realized that this country had many gangs, thugs, and desperadoes who carried concealed weapons and wouldn't think twice about using them. Shootouts with police were not uncommon. Thus, as I thought more about it, I concluded that perhaps the police were justified in carrying guns to protect themselves and the public.

As time went by, I fully comprehended the scope of America's crime problems, especially in its big cities. Homicides, bank robberies, property-related crimes, rape, assault, and battery were rampant. I also realized that this was a litigious society where others will sue you at the drop of a hat. People were obsessed with filing lawsuits and the abundance of lawyers willing to litigate these cases on a contingency-fee basis made it very easy. I was reminded over and over to be very cautious in how I dealt with my neighbors, fellow workers, business owners—even friends and relatives. They would not hesitate to sue you if you in some way, no matter how slight, violated their legal, property, civil, or privacy rights or in some manner happened to cause any personal injury. I was told that everyone was out to make extra money by winning a lawsuit. Children were suing their parents, parents were suing their ex-employers, employers were suing their competitors, business partners were suing one another, and neighbors were at odds and suing one another. The courts were jammed with civil and criminal cases; judges were overwhelmed and lawyers were doing lucrative business..

It did not take me long to notice that there was a huge difference between the British system of administration of laws, which I had studied, and the American legal system. American jurisprudence had evolved over two centuries. There was a range of things that differed between the two systems. There were difference in the sources of law, in the way the court system was set up, in the way the judges were appointed, and vast differences in the administration of justice. A few of the things that had impressed me most were the system of jury trials and the alternative dispute resolution system in civil cases such as mediation, arbitration, and case evaluations. The different court tier systems used by state courts and federal courts and the manner in which the judges were appointed also impressed me.

Since the legal system of this country is so complex, vast, and varied, some basic knowledge of the system will empower a new immigrant so that he will at least know the framework if he becomes entangled in it.

Basis of the American Legal System

The original basis of the laws of the country is the United States Constitution. The Constitution is the framework under which each of the three different branches of the government operates. The Constitution also grants the basic civil rights to the citizens and serves as the supreme law of the land. The Constitution grants to the federal government certain specific powers, such as declaring war, raising armies, regulating interstate and foreign commerce, and several others. The powers that are not specifically delegated to the federal government are given to the fifty states. The United States is divided into two sovereign forms of government: the government of the United States and the government of its fifty states.

The men who wrote the Constitution of the United States established these two levels of government in an attempt to prevent the centralization of power. No one group should have too much power at any one time. They strongly believed that absolute power corrupts absolutely. The writers of the Constitution intended to establish a limited national government.

Under this system, the states retain significant authority and autonomy. The Constitution of each of the fifty states contains many similar provisions to those in the US Constitution. If there is a conflict between federal and state laws, then most of the time, the state laws will be declared invalid.

Criminal Law versus Civil Law

This is very important to understand since the burden of proof is different for these two types of law. Criminal laws are those sets of laws designed to punish parties for violating the provisions of the penal code. Murder, burglary, robbery, assault, battery, and larceny are crimes committed against persons and property.

Violators of these laws commit crimes against society. Criminal actions are started against the alleged perpetrator by the state on behalf of the people or by the federal attorneys in federal courts.

All citizens of the United States are guaranteed certain rights during their criminal investigations and trials. Police officers and investigators are obliged to follow certain procedures in order to protect the accused's rights guaranteed by the Constitution. Among the most fundamental right is that all accused are presumed innocent until the prosecution proves them guilty "beyond all reasonable doubt."

On the other hand, civil law has different connotations. This is the type of law that defines rights between private parties. The investigation and evidentiary procedure that must be followed in civil cases are less stringent than those in criminal cases are. Civil cases usually involve resolution of disputes between private parties in such cases as personal injury, breach of contract, property disputes, and resolution of domestic disputes. The burden of proof in civil cases is on the preponderance of evidence, meaning that the claimant only has to adduce evidence to convince the court that but for defendant's negligence or recklessness, he would not have been injured or his property would not have sustained any damage.

The Court System

The greatest number of cases is prosecuted in the state and local courts. The federal courts are utilized to hear non-criminal and civil cases. Some federal crimes, such as terrorism and drug trafficking, are also dealt with in federal courts. The federal court system has the Supreme Court, which is the paramount court of the land. Its decisions are final and cannot be appealed.

State Courts

State courts hear the overwhelming majority of criminal and civil cases. Its decisions can be reviewed by courts of appeal and as a last resort the state's Supreme Court. Some unique cases can be appealed to the US Supreme Court.

Many state courts have small claims courts. Small claims courts are very important for ordinary small disputes. Attorneys are not allowed in this court and there are simple procedures for filing cases and getting it heard. Normally it has jurisdiction to award damages up to $7,500. Lots of ordinary citizens utilize this court for small legal matters of contention.

Judges

Federal judges are nominated by the president and subject to approval by a two-third vote of the Senate. To ensure their impartiality and to remove outside political pressures, they are appointed for life and can only be removed by impeachment or conviction of serious crimes.

At the state and local level, judges may be appointed or elected to specific terms of office. Elected or appointed judges at every level must be seen as impartial decision makers. Judges at state and local levels cannot be removed until their term has expired or by impeachment.

Since government agencies at federal, state, and local levels have broad responsibilities for conducting a range of programs, many of these courts have administrative law judges to resolve disputes. Administrative law judges usually hear cases involving workers compensation cases, health and welfare benefits, and domestic disputes.

Words of Caution

If you get entangled in serious criminal matters and are accused of committing a crime—no matter how petty the charges are—you should first ask for a public defender to defend you. Of course, this is only an option if you qualify. Your income and assets will be taken into consideration. Never plead guilty to the charges unless you've had an opportunity to consult an attorney. It may cost you few hundred dollars, but it will be worthwhile. Once you have good legal advice, take the next step.

Also get to know your Miranda Rights. This is one of the first rights that one must learn about the criminal system once you land in this country. This right prevents you from incriminating yourself if you confess to a crime at the time of your arrest or during interrogation by a police officer. The law does not require the police officer to read you your rights at the time of arrest. Police officers only need probable cause to arrest a person. However, before they start asking you questions about the alleged crime, police officers must read your Miranda rights to you. Essentially, the police officer must read to you as follows:

- You have the right to remain silent.
- Anything you say can be used against you in a court of law.
- You have the right to have an attorney present now and during any future questioning.
- If you cannot afford an attorney, one will be appointed for you free of charge if you so wish.

If you are arrested, you have the right to make one personal phone call to a family member or to your attorney.

The best approach to take if you are stopped by a police officer while driving or walking on the street or in your home is to produce your identification. Your driver's license or passport should suffice. Give the officer your full name and address and answer only those questions that are asked as briefly as possible. Do not volunteer any information. Do not argue with the police officer and try to cooperate as much as possible. If the officer orders you to put your arms up or get down on the ground, do so forthwith.

The police officers—especially in the big cities—are very well trained, highly intelligent, have state-of-the-art computers in their patrol cars, and have back up just few minutes away. Never think that you will be able to beat, deceive, or outsmart the police. Only criminal law attorneys with lots of experience should challenge the police officers if the case is prosecuted.

CHAPTER 14:
RAISING CHILDREN IN AMERICA

"The thing that impresses me most about America is the way the parents obey their children. Since the Second World War, many have observed the rise of child-centered as opposed to adult-centered families. Associated with this trend are such phenomena as the erosion of authority and proliferation of adults who have never had to grow up."

—Duke of Windsor, National Survey of Families, 1977

Many people in this country—as well as some living overseas who have visited this country—are of the firm belief that American society is not conducive for and the social environment not appropriate for raising healthy, happy, intelligent, well-rounded children. But is this really true? Is America a good place to bring up your family or not?

There is no one answer to this complex question. Much of it depends on the parents and how determined they are to raise their children the right way. It is undeniable, however, that the culture of the nation that you live in (in this case, America) will certainly have an impact on your kids' upbringing. In a recent

85

survey, nearly half of the parents said that they worry more about protecting their children from negative social influences than they do about paying their bills or having enough to eat every night. This is causing parents a lot of stress and tension. Parents, if both are working, do not have much time and energy to focus on their children's needs. Some researchers report that, in the past thirty years, the average time spent by parents with their children has dropped by 40 percent. This is mainly because both parents have to work to meet their family's needs and to earn money to educate their children. We often hear that American parents are either at work, sleeping, or resting to recharge themselves for the next day's work. The few leisure hours that they do have are usually spent doing household chores, cooking, cleaning, and running errands. During the weekends, parents usually go shopping, run errands, wash and iron, and enjoy their hobbies. This leaves just a few hours a week to devote to their children. Full-time stay-at-home moms and dads are very scarce these days.

This sort of revelation is very demoralizing to immigrant parents since a high percentage will tell you that they have come to this country for the sake of their children. They are willing to make all sorts of sacrifices and work hard to make sure that their children receive a college education and then advance in their chosen careers. This is their dream—and this is what motivates many to leave their motherland.

However, once they have lived here for few years, they realize that the success of their children will depend on their income, parental work pattern, their kids' proficiency in English, and things such as health insurance, child care, and support from teachers.

Since I am an optimist and having raised two kids myself, I strongly believe that wonderful, loving, caring, intelligent, successful kids are being raised in this country. I see them everywhere and I see the twinkle in the eyes of their proud parents. Almost every day,

I hear that the immigrant's children are doing very well in school, at work, in colleges, in professional fields, and in the sports arena. They are products and testament to a happy childhood and great upbringing by their parents.

According to my experience, there are eight pivotal areas that parents need to focus on during the first twelve formative years of their children. Once these octagonal fronts are confronted and conquered, the rest should be easy sailing. These goals could be very challenging but with patience, understanding and love they can be accomplished.

Children Have Many Legal Rights

One may have heard that parents are not allowed to even softly slap their children in America. If they do and the child calls the police or the Child Protection Services (CPS), the parents can end up in lot of trouble. Some parents even had to spend some time in jail because of this. Children under the age of eighteen are afforded basic rights by the Constitution enshrined by the Fourteenth Amendment. Researchers in this field have identified certain rights for children and it can be categorized into two groups:

- Economic, social, and cultural rights. This group of rights focuses on meeting the basic human needs, such as right to food, shelter, education, health care, and gainful employment.
- Environmental, cultural, and developmental rights. These are sometimes called "third-generation rights." It empowers children to live in a safe, healthy environment and they should be encouraged to foster their cultural, political, and economic abilities.

In America, parents have to be extremely careful that they do not neglect or physically abuse their children. Parents must respect their children's freedom of choice and not punish them in any physical manner. One must always keep in mind that children have certain rights in this country and those basic rights must be respected.

Teach Your Culture

Immigrant parents from different backgrounds and cultures always want their children to grow up with full knowledge and understanding of their culture. There is a strong presumption that kids who understand their own culture and practice it turn out to be better individuals when they become adults.

However, what many immigrant parents have experienced is that children do not take interest in their culture until they are teenagers and then they start to adopt whatever culture suits their lifestyle. The good thing is that most of the children live at home while attending high school. In this way, the parents can exert a strong influence on them. When they leave home and go to college, the real problem of neglecting one's culture begins. This is the case in most of the homes that I have seen.

In order to overcome this type of departure from one's culture, parents should start teaching their culture and traditions to their kids from the time they are one or two years old. Expose your kids to as many cultural and religious ceremonies as you can. Take them to all of the religious and cultural functions that you attend, teach them the ways and means of doing their rituals, and teach them how they can be culturally refined if they take interest in their heritage and culture. Get involved in church or temple activities. Children first learn from their parents and then they absorb whatever the surrounding environment has to offer. However, one has to be careful; parents cannot be excessively overbearing, controlling, or demanding. Trust and respect will do wonders if it is clearly shown to children by their parents.

Children Must Learn To Speak and Write English

If an immigrant parent wants their children to prosper and flourish in this country, the kids must learn to speak and write American English. This can be learned from a very early age. In schools all over the country, there are special classes for children to learn English as a second language. English can be learned in numerous ways, such as listening to the radio, attending private classes at local community colleges, having good interactions with American friends, going to church, and listening to elders who have been in the country for a long time. Practice makes perfect. There is nothing wrong in being bilingual and sometimes it is a major advantage—especially when looking for a good job. However, a lot of emphasis should be placed on learning to speak and write English. Have plenty of English books, music, and DVDs in your home. If you are proficient in English, try to speak English with your children as much as you can. The problem that looms large is that that almost half of immigrant parents have difficulty speaking English. This is not a good scenario. Many children, when they first go to elementary school, hardly have had any exposure to English. This is mainly because their parents hardly speak any English themselves. This type of situation is a huge disadvantage for the children who are starting school.

Recognizing and Dealing with Negative Peer Pressure

By the time kids reach ten or eleven, one will have to get used to peer pressure. If your child comes to you and says that he or she needs a very expensive, weird designer jacket, hip shoes that will cost an arm and a leg, or a BMW, you should immediately know that something is not right. If you ask your child why he or she wants those shoes when there are a dozen shoes in his closet and he says that it is because his or her friends have them and they look cool, you will know that peer pressure is getting to your child. Peer pressure can be defined as influence exerted by a peer group, encouraging a person to change his or her behavior, attitudes, and values in order to conform to group norms. Negative peer pressure can cause people to do things that they would not normally do. This includes things such as taking drugs, smoking, or buying items that they do not need. A lot of teens succumb to peer pressure and do things completely opposite of what they have been taught during their formative years. This culture is prevalent in high schools since students want to associate themselves in groups and the desire is to be popular. Adolescence is the time in life for experimentation. Thus, children will try to do things just to be part of the crowd—no matter what the costs are and no matter how bizarre the activity is. However, it ought to be remembered that peer pressure can also be of positive, wholesome influence. The positive influence could be when kids want to join a debating class, the football team, a cultural club, or want to volunteer.

The essential thing to remember is that parents must recognize and understand that children find it very hard to turn down the overtures being made by their friends and the popular kids in their school. Kids like to imitate and follow their friends' suggestions and ideas. The best way to handle the child who has gone overboard is to immediately take some positive steps to bail out your kid.

One can start by meeting with their friends and friends' parents to see what their views are. You can talk to your kids about peer pressure and how it can lead them into deep trouble. You can demonstrate how their demeanor and behavior can lead them into trouble with the law. You can impress upon them how vices such as drugs and alcohol can get them involved in auto accidents, how it can affect their grades, and other things that are negatively affecting them. This could include things such as staying awake during nights worrying about them or fearing a knock on the door by a policeman.

If you think that your child has gone off track in a bad way, do not be afraid to seek professional help from counselors, family elders, priests, or someone who your child respects. Peer pressure can ruin your kid's life. It has to be taken very seriously by the parents. It has to be nipped in the bud.

Understand That American Society Is Very Permissive

One of the most glaring things that new immigrants, especially from Third World countries, will notice when they arrive in this country will be how permissive and tolerant the American society is. Everyone is doing their own thing and, as long as they do not harm anyone else, it is accepted. Permissive society is a label given to a society where social norms are seen as very liberal and it is a major departure from what we normally do in our lives.

Since most of the immigrants reside in metropolitan areas, the permissive society is more obvious and prevalent. Since the whole mentality of the society is permissive, liberal, and tolerant, youngsters think it is all right to have girlfriends and boyfriends at a very early age. They also think that it is cool to have sex and use drugs and alcohol, and that it is all right to have abortions. Adolescents will readily endorse the gay lifestyle, living together without getting married, and so on.

For some of the more sophisticated, liberal immigrants who are accustomed to these permissive ways of thinking, it is probably acceptable for their kids to practice these liberal ways. However, for many people, this sort of lifestyle is abhorrent, especially if a person has strong religious and moral values. Parents usually do not want their children to have loose moral and social values. When parents resist, children rebel. This is where there could be a major difference in the thinking of parents and their kids. It could lead to major confrontation and some nasty fights.

The way to avoid this is to let your kids know your views and opinions while they are still in infancy. Place emphasis on the moral and religious values, on the fact that the divorce rate is very high in America, and that—to a high degree—family breakdowns can be attributed to the so-called permissive society. Be clear about the fact that for some people it is all right to adopt and live a liberal lifestyle, but that there is a right place and time for it. Stress the fact that as long as they are living under your roof and as long as you (the parents) are paying for their education and well-being, they have to obey your commandments.

Once they are eighteen and live and work on their own, the parents have no control. That is when they can do things according to their own choice and wishes. Once this message is relayed loud and clear, kids usually think twice about having a permissive lifestyle while living under their parents' roof. The message can be relayed in a loving and sensitive manner.

Babysitters and Grandparents

Immigrant parents will find that a good babysitter who is licensed by the county and works well caring for kids is usually very expensive. Some babysitters can charge as much as $200 a week per child, depending on how many hours they have to take care of your child. Many babysitters have rules and regulations that need to be obeyed, such as giving your youngsters medicine, putting them to sleep, and feeding them. Some of them just do not know how to give tender love and care to your kids. Some do not know what to do in emergencies, such as earthquakes or fires. It is important to do a thorough background check of the babysitter before employing them. All counties keep records of these licensed babysitters and one can find out about any licensed babysitter by calling your local social welfare office. The point that needs to be made here is not to expect your babysitter to raise your kids. Lots of parents think that, since they are paying the babysitter, the sitter must teach the kids the pros and cons of life and discipline and all vices and virtues. That is asking too much. The parents should play that role and should not assign it to anyone else.

Many kids are being raised by their grandparents in America these days since lots of two-parent homes do not exist. Since the divorce rate is high and family breakups are quite common, the children suffer. Mothers often get custody of the children. Since mothers have to go to work to earn money, they usually leave their children with their parents. Statistics reveal that more than 25 percent of school-aged children are being raised by their grandparents. This is not fair to the children or to the grandparents. The grandparents actually have done their part by raising their own children and during their golden years, they do not want to be burdened with this extra hassle and responsibility. Secondly, grandparents love and adore their grandchildren and chances are good that they will do and buy things that will spoil them. Thirdly, many grandparents do not have extra money to spend on their grandchildren because they have to live on a limited budget. Fourthly, grandparents usually have health concerns of their own and need time to rest and do things according to their own schedule rather than programming their lives around their grandkids. Lastly, grandparents should not be made to feel badly because they cannot contribute their time, energy, and money to raise their grandkids. They should live their own lives in retirement.

This built-in grandparent babysitting should be carefully thought out and done only as a last resort. The same applies to leaving your children with any family member. Many family members take advantage of these situations and family squabbles and bickering are often the end result.

The Cost of Raising Children

A frightening statistics is that it costs about $250,000 to raise a child from the time they are born until they reach the age of eighteen. It is not going to be fun to raise two kids if the parents are only earning $18 or $22 per hour—or much less. The price tag is discouraging lots of young married couples from having children. Some would rather have pets. This is a sad commentary on American society. One of the reasons it has become so outrageously expensive is because the parents have become accustomed to buying designer clothes and shoes and have to give them what the other kids from wealthy families have. A college education is very expensive. Children make outrageous demands and some poor parents have to oblige. If they don't, they have depressed, unhappy kids in the house. Keeping up with the peers is damaging to the family budget as well as to the morale of the family.

Balancing Work and Family

If both parents work, there are increased demands on them to balance work and family life. About twenty-five years ago, work and family balance used to be just the woman's role. However, these days, men are just as likely to have difficulty in managing work and family demands. Careful consideration needs to be made when looking for work. What comes first? Money or children? Who is going to cook, feed, clean, wash, and do other household chores? Who is going to tend to the needs of the children? Who is going to take the kids to sports practices? Who is going to attend parent-teacher conferences? Who is going to take the kids to the doctor or dentist? Many immigrants become deeply engrossed in their work. In the process, they forget about their own lives and that of their children. They find it difficult to find good balance. This is the reason why there is a strong relationship between the number of paid hours and work-family conflict, especially those with preschool children. Longer work hours by husbands have been shown to result in greater family conflict and higher divorce rates.

A good balance is necessary to raise healthy, happy children. Look for a job that allows flextime if your employer will allow that. Prioritize chores, set aside specific quality time with each child on a daily basis, and both spouses have to be flexible and have a plan of action with kids' interests in mind. Of equal importance is to have someone trustworthy to watch your children so that you and your spouse can have some time together as a married couple.

Working parents will always face challenges in managing their many responsibilities. Children and work have to be carefully considered and prioritized. By establishing personal priorities and communicating about their roles to one another, parents can achieve balance in their lives. This balancing act is important for raising children and for the parents to be able to live a normal, happy, and healthy married life.

After abiding with the cardinal principles that will help parents to raise capable, functioning human beings, the rest is up to the kids. The children will have to bear in mind that every choice they make in life will contribute to their growth or destruction. They must learn—from infancy—the importance of honesty, decency, responsibility, and compassion. These values will take them to greater heights in life. Skills in reading and math cannot develop the kind of citizens that we need for a more productive, humane society. Parents, teachers, and the entire village must help their children to become functioning adults.

Chapter 15:
The School System

"Education is the great engine of personal development. It is through education that a daughter of a peasant can become a doctor, that a son of a mineworker can become the manager of the mine, and child of a farm worker can become the president of a nation."

—Nelson Mandela

Having acquired a British education and having experienced the novelty of the British education system for more than eighteen years, I thought that there was no better system in the world. Under the British system, uniforms are a must, and well-trained government teachers are mandatory. Good discipline is emphasized and teachers receive great respect from children. The whole objective is to educate a student to a level where he or she can pass university qualification exams at the age of seventeen or eighteen. Light corporal punishment by the principal was tolerated during my time. Parents supported that policy. Primary education was mainly free, but starting with secondary education, school fees had to be paid. Parents had to buy books and uniforms. It was then left to the students to do their best and acquire the level of education that they wanted to achieve.

Despite heavy emphasis on education by parents and lots of encouragement from family, friends, and teachers, only about 10 percent of students could proceed to college-level education. This was because the system would flush them out by failing them in the major exams or, if they did pass, the parents would not have money and resources to send their children for higher education. For higher college education, one had to go abroad since there were few universities. Government grants, scholarships, and private sponsors were few. Grants and scholarships were given to the lucky few who were children of well-known people or were extremely bright and had gained the attention of local politicians. Poor children with above-average grades were neglected. Some high school students had to drop out to find a job and to start financially supporting their families. Girls were given low priority by their parents since money had to be spent on boys to receive the best education. Girls were encouraged to leave school after completing eighth grade, and then they were kept home for a few years and taught basic household chores and cooking. Parents would then find a suitable suitor, and the daughters were expected to get married. That was the tradition back then. As always, there were exceptions, but in most families, this was the rule of the thumb.

Although it was very difficult for the poor kids to advance to tertiary education because their parents could not afford it, there were other sources for finding financial assistance, especially for the brightest and the cleverest. Religious organizations, churches, and charitable organizations would sometimes help poor students pay for fees and books.

There were not too many jobs available for the graduates and many students who went abroad for college never returned after graduation. This often created bitter feelings and deep regrets in the hearts of those who had sponsored the students financially and morally. The initial expectation of those sponsors was that the students would return to their country, serve their people, and become valuable members of society. Oftentimes, this did not happen.

When we first arrived in this country, education was not a concern. Since we both were literate, had a reasonably good command of the English language, and our daughter was just a baby, there was no need to inquire into the educational system.

As our daughters grew and reached school age, we began researching seriously. We found that schools could be found everywhere and that the United States has one of the largest universal education systems in the world. We found that the education system was primarily the responsibility of the state and the local governments. Unlike most other nations, the United States does not operate a national education system. The federal government does not approve any curriculum. Individual states have great control over what is taught in schools and what requirements a student must meet. There is variation from state to state as it relates to courses, subjects, and other activities. Some common things are standardized. Formal schooling lasts twelve years or until the child reaches eighteen. School attendance is compulsory for students. All children have access to free public schools. Some private schools are available, but students are required to pay tuition. Many of these private schools are run by churches and other religious organizations. More than half of the nation's private school students attend Catholic schools. Other private schools reflect America's religious diversity. Many parents home school their children under guidelines established by each state.

All primary and secondary education is referred to as K–12 education. The majority of children begin education around the age of six. The parents that can afford to usually send their kids to kindergarten prior to starting the elementary school. After elementary school, children enter middle school, and then high school. In high school, there is a wide variety of subjects that students can take. They have to earn a certain number of credits in order to graduate and be awarded a diploma. There is no final examination as in many other countries.

A high school diploma is necessary for enrolling in post-secondary education. Many colleges and universities require the students to pass with good marks on SAT (Scholastic Achievement Test) before they can be enrolled into their institution. The SAT exam is supposed to give students an equal opportunity to enter college irrespective of family background, inconsistent grade system and curriculum standards in the nation's high schools. Thus, if a student wants to go to a prestigious college, he must do extremely well in the SAT exams.

The thing that I like about the American school system is that it also offers non-academic options. For example, almost all schools offer different types of sports. Most high schools offer sports throughout the year. Football, baseball, basketball, golf, swimming, and tennis are available to students as part of the non-academic curriculum. After school, students are encouraged to attend art, chess, debate, cultural, and other similar clubs to keep their minds occupied and to keep them off the streets. Even summer schools are available to those kids who want to steer clear of crime, drugs, and gangs.

Parents need to know that their children have to start preparing for college very early in their high school years. To get into good colleges, students have to take courses in subjects that will make them eligible to enroll in good colleges. For example, some colleges require only two years of math, but others will require three or four years of math. Early preparation for college should be kept in mind by parents and kids.

The other major problem that parents will have to face is how to finance their kids' education. College education has become very expensive and can cost close to $50,000 per year for food, board, tuition, books, and transportation. The top students get scholarships. These kids are usually very gifted and always rank in the top 10 percent of their class. However, some get scholarships if they excel in sports—even if their grades are average. Grants are available from federal and state governments. These do not have to be repaid. Loans are also available with low interest rates that have to be paid back once the students graduate. There are several other sources of education funding, such as federal work-study. Many students finance themselves as they go by taking part-time work and staying with their parents until they finish their education.

Today, American schools are more ethnically diverse; Latin American and Asian students are quickly filling the classrooms. It is fairly common to find schools where more than a dozen different languages are taught—from Arabic to Vietnamese.

Despite their decentralization and diversity, public schools remain cohesive in how they are operated. A student transferring from California to New Jersey will find some differences, but the academic subjects are very similar.

Our daughter Suhani went through the education system and, on the whole, we were satisfied with the standard of education that she received. She graduated from the state university with a four-year degree. The thing that we liked most about her education was that by the time she finished college, she had become a well-rounded, independent thinker and a good advocate of her thoughts and actions. She is well versed in English, well rehearsed in social sciences, and articulates her thoughts and expressions very well.

We also had the opportunity to become deeply involved in the special education that was given to our special-needs-challenged daughter, Cahani. She also attended the public school system, but always was registered in the special education classes. We found that her curriculum was adequate. The teachers were qualified and used lots of patience and specialized techniques to teach the kids according to their mental and physical abilities. We feel fortunate to be living in this country where children with disabilities are given a full education to make them independent in daily living as well as to bolster their self-esteem.

The American education system still provides a good quality education. Numerous world leaders, presidents, and prime ministers are the product of American education. In many fields and industries, the American education system offers the most progressive, sought-after programs at the world's best schools. America is one country where interested students can pursue anything from nuclear science to film and dance courses. American education possibilities are almost endless.

Chapter 16:
What I Like About Living in the United States

If you live in America, you are in one of—if not *the*—best country most capable of weathering the economic storm. Compared to many other countries, wages in the United States are quite high and many people go to live in the United States in order to make more money than they have before. By immigrating to the United States, you can provide your family with a lifestyle that you have only ever dreamed of before. Getting a visa to live in America could be described as nothing other than a life-changing experience.

Every year nearly one million people immigrate to the United States. Despite the fact that the US economy is in the doldrums right now, people still are lining up to emigrate to this country. The United States continues to be a magnet for immigrants and those newcomers contribute immensely to American life just as the earlier generations did. What is the magnet? What is pulling them to this country? Why do they want so desperately to come and live here despite the faltering economy? I am certain, if a poll was taken all over the world, we will find that hundreds of million people on this earth would love to emigrate to the United States.

People migrate for different reasons. Some come here to get wealthy by hard work. Some come here to advance their careers. Some come to settle here for the sake of their children. However, most come here to become wealthy and prosperous and enjoy a good standard of living. I can't speak for others, but I can describe why I came here in the first place and why I have fallen in love with this country. It has become my home, and I feel so very fortunate to live here and to be a part of America. In that regard, I am certain that I am of the same mindset of nearly all immigrants. I came to this country to attain the American Dream. My definition of the American Dream is the belief that, through hard work, determination, and drive, a person in this country, no matter what his status was when he first arrived here, can better the quality of his life in terms of financial prosperity and personal freedom. Anyone in this country can get a share of America's immense wealth through hard work and sacrifices. This was my belief when I first set foot in this country and I feel the same today.

You may not like this country when you first get here. The American way of doing things may look and sound odd and the hustle and bustle may be overwhelming. Your first job may not be to your liking. You probably do not like the food, the jammed freeways, the customs, and the traditions. Even popular sports may be somewhat confusing at times. Whatever one does not like has to be tolerated—and it takes time to get used to it. The fact remains that most immigrants like this country and very few return to their homeland.

Here is the list of things that I have come to like about the United States of America. The list is in random order and is not conclusive since the longer I live in this country, the more things I like.

The Land of Opportunity

This is the country where one can fulfill dreams and aspirations with hard work, ingenuity, and the exercise of wisdom. America provides everyone with a level playing field when one is born. It is up to the individual to decide how well to do in life. The education system has a broad curriculum and teaches the basics of attaining a good life and a high standard of living. Once a student gets a college education, the opportunities have no boundaries. If a person wants to become a rocket scientist, there are programs and education guidelines to follow. If one wants to learn a trade, there are programs and training available. If one wants to become a professional athlete, there are programs that provide the skills and knowledge to become a professional player, provided you have the right talents. If one wants to be a clerk, then that option is open. If one wants to become a superstar actor, there are ways and means to achieve that. The national government policies and corporate philosophy are formulated to make a human being achieve his or her maximum potential. The only requirement is hard work, desire, and ambition to get to the top. A little bit of luck is needed and sometimes the right opportunity has to be awaited for. Women have broken the glass ceiling to become CEOs and presidents of huge corporations. People from different origins have become successful businessmen, politicians, lawyers, doctors, engineers, and teachers and can be found in every career. People from different countries have been given opportunities to become astronauts, rocket scientists, prominent politicians, heads of corporations, and important military personnel. There are no limits to what one can do and achieve.

Freedoms

Freedoms such as speech, press, religion, travel, and the right to a jury trial are guaranteed by the US Constitution as well as by state constitutions. Perhaps this is one of the best reasons to live in this country. One is free to give an opinion on any topic that is bothering a person. There is nothing in this country to stop a person from sharing an opinion about any issue. If you want to condemn your government, it is all right. If you want to condemn your politicians, it is all right. If you want to criticize or question the policies or competence your school administrators, you may do that. If you want to demonstrate, march, parade, or protest, it is going to be accommodated by your city or county—provided you take out a permit. And, permits are readily given. The government has some wide guidelines, but it is very permissive. There are no prior restraints in demonstration of your ideas and opinions.

One has the freedom to practice religion in any fashion. No one has the right to question a person about the rites and rituals of a person's religion or how it is being practiced. Among the developed countries, the United States is one of the most religious in terms of demographics. A majority of the people in one survey disclosed that religion played a very important role in their lives. It is quite common to see a church, a Hindu temple, a mosque, and a synagogue built in the same general area of a city or a town. Atheists and agnostics are given their respective rights in the community. Gays have many rights that are not found in many advanced, liberal countries.

There are other freedoms and rights highly respected by the government. The protection of its citizens by the Due Process clause found in the Fifth and Fourteenth Amendments of the US Constitution guarantees that no person shall be deprived of "life, liberty, and property without due process of law." Due process essentially means that the laws must be fair and reasonable, must be made in compliance with the Constitution, and must apply equally to everyone.

There are very few places on this planet where these sorts of human rights and privileges are bestowed and entrusted to the citizens of the country. President Abraham Lincoln once greatly inspired his people when he stated "I leave you hoping that the lamp of liberty will burn in your bosoms until there shall no longer be a doubt that all men are created free and equal."

Free Markets

The competition of our market results in the creation of highly efficient businesses that deliver necessary products and services to consumers. Competition promotes innovation, bringing down the prices of goods and services and making them affordable. The variety of available goods is also something that this country has to offer at relatively cheap prices. For example, if one wants to purchase a laptop, there is a wide range of makes, models, and prices. One can buy a laptop for $450 or pay as much as $3,500. It is similar for groceries, clothing, furniture, and appliances.

The free market system also encourages good customer service and quality control. We can expect courteous service from retail clerks to government workers serving the needs of the public. This competitive spirit somewhat eliminates the issue of bribery and favoritism from the general equation of doing business in this country. The free market economy also encourages the benefits of supply and demand economy. When the demand exceeds supply, prices can be raised but when supply is more than the demand-than the prices have to be reduced. This encourages comparison shopping by the consumers. The customer is always the king and should be able to get the best price for his desired merchandize.

Cultural Diversity

There are people living and working in this country who are from every corner of the earth. This is a great country to meet people from all over the world. Most of the neighborhoods have people from Latin America, Asia, the Philippines, Europe, and Africa living next to American-born natives. They all appreciate and respect one another's cultures, traditions, and ways of achieving useful purpose in their daily lives. If you go downtown or to a mall, you are bound to find restaurants serving different cuisine from different countries. If you go shopping, you will see retail clerks from different countries serving your needs. If you go to government departments, you will find people of all nationalities serving you. They may have different accents, appearances, religions, or diets, but they are all Americans. I can go to any sports event and see a rainbow of people enjoying the game. I can go to movie theater and decide whether I want to see a Hollywood movie or a Bollywood movie or an Asian movie. I can go to a local arts center and see art displays from all over the world.

This diversity reflects a tolerant society; it reflects a rich society and, most of all, it reflects that people from all over the world can stand united together with a strong sense of national pride.

Scientific Advancements and Innovations

The people of this country are innovative and are always searching and inventing things that will make life much easier. How many times have we heard that some brilliant scientist has found a new drug to cure this disease or the other? This is a great country where things such as new medicine, drugs, electronics, software, cars, or useful home gadgets are invented, tried, and tested—and then sold to the masses. There is genuine fondness for scientific advancement and technological innovation in the hearts and minds of the American people. Strong scientific areas include nuclear research, space programs, military research, and biotech. Inventors such as Thomas Edison, Alexander Graham Bell, and Henry Ford helped build America's unparalleled scientific and technological dominance. America became a nation of invention in the twentieth century. Of more than 530 Nobel laureates in physics, chemistry, or medicine since 1901, more than 200 have been Americans. Ideas that were developed in leading universities and the labs of major corporations became products for Ford, IBM, Boeing, Intel, and Google. The federal government spends billions of dollars every year in research and development of new medicines, drugs, and technological advancement in science and engineering.

A Highly Planned and Organized Country

It could be that America is so highly structured and organized because it is a relatively new country. It has great infrastructure. The roads and freeways, park systems, malls, housing developments, and utilities are all carefully designed, planned, constructed, and organized so that the public may get the maximum use out of them. The network of roads and freeways and the manner in which they are constructed with wide lanes, shoulders, barriers, and excellent signage are the best in the world. The safety of motorists is of utmost importance. Saving lives on the road is extremely important to the government.

Housing developments are well planned with ample parking, proximity to schools, parks, libraries, freeways, and malls, making life easier for everyone. Nice parks, golf courses, and swimming pools are always close for people to enjoy. You might have to pay for some of these facilities, but they are there. If you want to use them, they are available.

Municipal governments, business owners, and local garbage companies work hard to keep the streets clean and beautiful with trees and center islands and the sidewalks in good repair. These local efforts plus laws and regulations relating to hygiene, give the country an aura of class and makes it a desirable place to live, work, and to raise a family.

Natural Beauty

The natural beauty of America is beyond description. Mountains, rivers, lakes, coastlines, valleys, peaks, Yosemite Park, the Yellowstone Park, and the Grand Canyon are just a few examples of this country's natural beauty. The Mount Rainer National Park, Niagara Falls, and the Hawaii Volcanoes National Park will all take your breath away when you see them for the first time. One can enjoy this country's natural beauty in a variety of ways. Camping, hiking, and leisurely driving are possible in all of these beautiful parks. Nature preservation laws and regulations keep the natural beauty of this country intact and delight one's mind and soul with every visit. The federal and state governments spend billions of dollars to preserve these natural environments.

There are many states in this country where a person can easily go skiing in winter and go to the ocean for surfing and picnicking in the summer. A plethora of natural recreational areas are within driving distance and one does not have to spend too much money to get to these splendid places to enjoy the natural beauty of this country. Some of the national parks charge a twenty-dollar fee, but that money is spent to maintain the park roads and camping sites.

A Great Country to Retire

This country takes care of its elderly retired people. It is a great country to retire—provided one has some retirement income, some savings as well as beneficiary of Social Security, which one becomes eligible for after the age of sixty-two. Elderly people have a lot of civil rights since the passing of Americans for Disabilities Act. They are taken care of in nursing homes in a relatively nice manner. Nursing homes are highly regulated and kept in check by the state and county health regulators. The elderly are given comfortable accommodations, meals, and nursing care if they decide to move into private nursing homes. In fact, the high standard of medical care provided to elderly people and their general happiness during their golden years is one of the reasons why longevity in the United States is hovering around eighty— and higher for women. Organizations such as the AARP lobby for elderly people's rights and keep abreast of changing health-care laws. It also provides assistance to the elderly relating to any welfare issues.

Great Sporting Nation

This country has a great affinity for sports. Every man, woman, and child has at least one sport that they truly love. They either actively participate or watch the sport and cheer for their team as a hardcore fan. Numerous sports have a unique American signature, such as football and baseball. Basketball, soccer, ice hockey, golf, and tennis have been imported, but have built up a great fan base. Some even think that cheerleading is a sport and needs to be appreciated as such. The participants are great athletes. Americans spend billions of dollars in promoting and fostering their sports teams. Professional players are paid as much as two hundred million dollars for three years and some are paid even more by their sponsors. Many Americans spend at least a quarter of their leisure time watching their favorite sport on TV or practicing and playing the game. During the winter months, they spend more time watching football than any other sport. Football widows are women during winter months whose husbands and kids are always engrossed in their own sports. Although it has become expensive to go to some of these professional sporting events,

Americans enjoy their sports. That is the reason why Americans do so well in Olympics and other international sporting events.

The recent announcement about holding The America's Cup yachting competition in San Francisco, California in 2013 has generated a new passion and interest for this acclaimed water sport. It is an international sport in which the United States always has major stake and world's top sailors and yacht designers usually participate. The wealthy entrepreneurs and sponsors' have made this sport a symbol of American pride and honor.

Sports are entertaining, good for physical fitness, and great for mental gymnastics. They also provide a wonderful feeling of contentment and time to replenish the energy and strength that are exerted during the week at work and dealing with life. Kindergarteners are taught the value of playing at least one sport. It builds character, teaches teamwork, and keeps kids occupied in a constructive manner. Above all, it is great for physical fitness. In schools and colleges, sports play a major part. Some colleges even give extra credit to kids who are good players.

I like sports because they are entertaining and give me time to enjoy something with my wife and family. There are six professional sports franchises in my hometown: two football, two baseball, one basketball, and one ice hockey team. The stadiums are located within driving distance of my home and if I am interested in attending any of their games, tickets are readily available. Although I do not spend too much money in entertaining myself by attending major sporting events, over the years I have attended many professional sporting events and fully enjoyed them. There is good fun to be derived from tailgating, betting on your favorite sports team, and discussing certain games with your fellow workers and friends about the performance of your favorite players. America is a Mecca for sports.

The System of Checks and Balances

The American Constitutional system includes a notion known as the separation of powers. Under this system, the federal government is divided into three branches: legislative, executive, and judicial. These three branches are not independent of one another because the Constitution set up a system of checks and balances to ensure that no branch became too powerful. It also encourages cooperation between branches as well as fostering debates on controversial issues. "Ambition must be made to counteract ambition," wrote James Madison, one of the founding fathers.

The system of checks and balances requires Congress and the president to work together if they are determined to accomplish something. This system has worked very well for more than two centuries during peace and war, depression and prosperity—despite the fact that some huge clashes have occurred relating to some controversial issues. One just has to know that the legislative branch makes the laws and keeps a check over the executive branch. The executive branch carries out the laws. The legislative branch can override the presidential vetoes with a two-thirds vote. The executive branch has checks over the legislative branch. It has veto powers and has powers to call special sessions of Congress. The judicial branch is given power to interpret laws. It keeps a check over the executive branch in that courts can judge executive actions to be unconstitutional. Judges, once appointed, are there for life.

This system prevents corruption and favoritism—and prevents unscrupulous people from holding key positions in government. It prevents dictatorship. The legislative branch has impeachment powers to remove unfit presidents—and has done so on a few occasions.

Great People

The majority of the American-born people are a very open-minded and happy-go-lucky bunch. They are hardworking and generous. They are always ready to help strangers. If there is a natural disaster anywhere in the world, American volunteers, Red Cross workers, doctors, firefighters, and military personnel are the first to respond. They will give up their vacation times, paychecks, and family to go overseas and help the victims. If there is any catastrophe at home, such as 9/11, Hurricane Katrina, earthquakes, tornadoes, or fires, Americans are always opening their pockets, and donations come pouring in. One report shows that American people privately donate thirty four billion dollars overseas. Furthermore, non government organizations supplies six and half billion dollars in goods, grants and volunteers.

They believe in hard work during weekdays, playing hard on their days off, and having fun in life. They have a great sense of humor and most of them believe in diversity, cohesiveness, and patriotism. As long as you do not step on their toes and violate their rights, they are willing to tolerate anything from anyone. At the same time, they are very aggressive and assertive to protect their freedoms and their country. They are the kind of people who are always determined to handle things their own way. "I can handle it!" is a common attitude. No matter whether it is about losing a job, getting a divorce, or fighting a horrible disease, Americans do not lose hope. They will always say, "I can handle that." This kind of determination and resolve makes Americans, very strong-minded and hardy people.

Patriotism is embedded in every American's heart and soul. They realize that Americans have the responsibility to preserve their freedoms, opportunities, and rights. They constantly try to do things that will preserve life, liberty, and the pursuit of happiness. Serving in the military, serving on the jury system, and voting in elections are taken by Americans as good ways to show patriotism. They are proud of their armed forces and are supportive of several wars that are being fought overseas in the name of liberation, freedom, and democracy. Several polls show that Americans would not prefer to live in any other country because they believe that they have the best system of government in the world. Only 7 percent of Americans stated that they would rather live in another country if given a choice.

Americans are very adventurous. Most of them have traveled widely—either during their school years or after their kids have grown and left home. Most of them have seen at least five states of their own vast country. Traveling and exploring in foreign countries is a great pastime for Americans.

They take great interest in preserving nature, the environment, and the many beautiful architectural wonders created by their ancestors. They are proud people—proud of their country, proud of their government, proud of their rate of progress and prosperity, proud of their freedom, and proud of their standard of living.

High Standard of Living

I thoroughly enjoy the standard of living in this great country. The standard of living in America is one of the highest in the world. It has always ranked in the top ten countries in the world as having the best standard of living.

The median income of approximately $43,000 per household is one of the highest in the world. Most of the homes have two income earners. The GDP is very high. Americans are some of the wealthiest people in the world. The material possessions that Americans own rank the highest in the world. Americans own more radios, televisions, and personal computers per capita than any country in the world. About 65 percent of Americans own their own homes.

The only gripe that I have in this regard is that America has one of the widest gaps between rich and poor. The capitalism system works in this country quite well and has made about 0.9 percent of the population super rich. They are billionaires. Some millionaires and billionaires are highly educated, top-level executives, celebrities, politicians, and Ivy League graduates. Some have inherited their wealth from family estates, but most of them are self-made millionaires. They worked hard, invested wisely, made sacrifices, had good luck on their side, and never gave up in times of adversity. Most of them are children of immigrants whose parents worked in factories or farms. They were taught the value of hard work and money. They were taught how to live in a frugal manner and they were taught how to invest by their educators. There are hundreds of millionaires who have stories of how they became prosperous by using their brains and by toiling day and night. America is one of the few countries where one will readily find a millionaire, a plumber, or an electrician driving a Lexus or a Mercedes. It is just that the plumbers and electricians are probably working twice as hard to maintain their standard of living.

America Is Still a Superpower

This is another reason why I like this country. America is still the world's only superpower. The government gives a person in this country a sense of security and protection. The military and economic power of this country is still the envy of the world. After the dissolution of the Soviet Union in 1991, America was the only superpower left. The military has the largest and most powerful armed forces in the world. Its air force is the best. The powerful military alliance with Western Europe (NATO) and the global intelligence network (CIA) give America an edge over other large countries, such as China and India.

The citizens of this country can go to sleep every night knowing full well that no hostile country will be able to drop a bomb on their city from thousands of miles away. The country is protected. The brave men and women of our armed forces are trained, equipped, and ready to give their lives for their country. The brave soldiers and airmen fighting in Iraq and Afghanistan are our heroes and we salute them with appreciation and gratitude.

There is no denial that our military expenditure is exorbitant—more than six hundred billion dollars per year. Americans do not mind since we strongly believe that, in order to preserve our freedom and democracy, we will have to spend money and sadly endure sacrifices of many young lives. Otherwise, some other country will become the super-power. We will have to live in constant fear and anxiety, especially when hostile countries have nuclear capabilities. It goes without any lamenting that every cent of our tax dollars spent on our military is worth it.

CHAPTER 17:
THINGS I DISLIKE ABOUT LIVING IN AMERICA

I am the first to confess that I do not like everything about this country. I must be honest that not everything that touches and affects my life in America meets my satisfaction. I wish that I had a magic wand and could change a few things about this society. A number of things about this country bothers me a lot, but as I grow older, I have accepted some of the things that used to irritate and concern me. Since I chose to live in this country, I have to accept and make peace with the good and the bad things that are happening all around me.

I also keep in mind that no place on the face of this earth offers absolute perfection. Nobody has figured it all out. No nation has developed a social and political system that eliminates all flaws. This is impossible because of the very nature of human beings. We are imperfect creatures, so it only stands to reason that the societies and nations that we build will be imperfect, too. Even under the best of circumstances.

Furthermore, consolation lies in the fact that other industrialized countries have similar problems and so, I really should not be complaining. I am going to list some things that are of concern to me. I am certain that my pet peeve list will be much different from the homeless men and women on the streets that are trying to figure out where their next dinner is going to come from. I am certain that if I tried harder, I could come up with more things in this country that I am unhappy about. However, I have no desire to trash my beloved country of choice.

Crime, Violence, and Drugs

People living in different parts of the world have a vision of the United States being a very safe, secure, and peaceful country. The American government fights all the wars outside its borders. To a great extent, this assumption is true. That is the reason why the United States attracts millions of tourists every year and most of them go to major cities. Most of these tourists have a good time, eat in numerous restaurants, go to malls, take field trips, stay in hotels and motels in different cities, and then return home safe, secure, and very happy. However, a few unfortunate ones do have bad experiences having to deal with thugs, thieves, and ruthless criminals.

There is another side to this. The reality is that the United States has been facing and battling with a rising number of crimes, gang activities, and drug problems for the last two decades. America has approximately seven million prisoners incarcerated in its prisons. This is the highest number of prisoners in any country in the world. The homicide rate is the highest when compared with similar industrialized countries. One statistic revealed that the homicide rate in the United States is near 5.5 for every 100,000 residents. This is excessively high. In similar industrialized countries, such as France and Germany, the ratio is 2.5 per 100,000.

The proliferation of unlicensed handguns, gang violence, drugs, and ruthless criminals are often quoted as the cause for these homicides. The victims are usually males younger than twenty-five and often minorities. This is very disturbing and despite state and local governments determined efforts to curtail these violent crimes, the criminals still seem to be winning. Serious crimes, such as rape, robbery, larceny, and aggravated assault, are on the rise in larger cities. Serious crime rates vary from state to state.

These crime statistics are disturbing. It is a shame that this great country cannot assure its citizens one hundred percent that they can walk the streets, especially in big cities, and be safe. The overhead cameras, the high presence of police officers, the three strikes laws, and serious punishments handed down by judges are not having a deterrent effect. It is my pious hope that, in time to come, law enforcement officers and the criminal court system will eventually have the upper hand over ruthless criminals. Criminals in this country carry powerful, unlicensed weapons and do not hesitate to use them. Big cities have to train and retain powerful police forces to apprehend and prosecute these criminals. Most cities are successful in doing that. Some cities allocate as much as 60 percent of their budget to fire and police departments.

One can do many sensible things to avoid becoming a victim of crime and they all require common sense. Some of the things that one may want to seriously consider are:

- Stay away from rough areas, especially at nighttime in big cities. Do not drive around in those areas unnecessarily.
- A high level of awareness is important. Be aware of your surroundings wherever you park your car and when you are getting into or out of your car.

- Stay in a group while walking down the streets, especially in large cities
- Carry your wallet in your front pocket and try to carry little cash.
- Do not leave your car keys in your car. If you get car-jacked, let the thieves have the car.
- If someone tries to rob you, hand over the money and run. Call the police when you feel safe.
- If you have car trouble, put out signals so that other motorists can see you. Stay inside your car, but first make sure it is parked in a safe place.

Identity Fraud

Identity fraud occurs when someone uses your personal information without your permission. They may use your name, Social Security number, or credit card number without your consent.

This crime is getting worse every year; as many as nine million people are affected every year. The nature of this crime is such that you may not know about it till you review your credit card statement or your credit report and you will notice the charges that you did not make. If you do not want to become a victim of this crime, you must always be vigilant and aware of your surroundings—and do not give your credit card numbers to anyone who you do not trust. Just be extra careful while using the ATM machines and purchasing stuff on the Internet with your credit card.

Materialism

You will only have to observe few high school students to notice how they are dressed. They wear fancy clothes and shoes and they have gadgets such as cell phones, iPods, designer backpacks, and cars. They do not want to be even a step behind their peers and have to keep up with modern trends and fashion. Their parents are the ones who have to suffer. Some parents take extra part-time work just to be able to buy modern and fashionable things for their children, especially for their high school kids. That is one of the reasons why America is seen as a very materialistic society. Our behavior is often selfish, self-indulgent, and egotistic.

One statistic shows that an average American household with two children spends more on high-end shoes, designer jeans, lipstick, and personal fitness trainers per year than on food. Sport utility vehicles, laptop computers, digital cameras, electronic personal organizers, cell phones, and expensive TVs have become absolute necessities. Many high school students will not go to school unless they have a car. Many will go without proper textbooks, but must have a state-of-the-art cell phone. According to American Mythos, a national survey found that 82 percent of Americans thought that they were materialistic and 77 percent said they were self-indulgent.

This is a sad commentary on the way we conduct our lives. The competition and trying to fulfill our selfish needs to impress our friends and relatives has gone too far in this country. Some people have a garage full of stuff that they really do not need. Clothes, shoes, electronic accessories, furniture, and books are piled ceiling high and most of them are in good condition. Many were bought and used once or twice, but when they went out of fashion, they were discarded—never to be used again.

Many church and civic leaders have spoken out on this topic. The youngsters are constantly told to be careful how and where they spend their money. It is slowly sinking in, but many still splurge. Political leaders can set examples by focusing less on themselves and their pockets and redirecting their energy toward making better lives for their constituents. Politicians can be great role models and trendsetters. By demonstrating their own simple living habits, they can at least start showing some signs of modesty to the younger generation.

Movie stars and people in entertainment business can also set examples by spending less on themselves and being less materialistic. They can do much more for their country by way of helping the poor, downtrodden, homeless, disabled, and handicapped.

The Gradual Breakdown of Family Life

America is quickly becoming a one-parent household society. Because of economic independence, stress, lack of mutual commitment between couples, and bickering about petty things, divorce rates have gone up drastically in the past two decades. The Americans for Divorce Reform estimates that "Probably 40 percent or possibly 50 percent of marriages will end up in divorce if current trends continue." The divorce rate for second marriages is even higher. Who suffers? Of course, it is the children. The kids are suffering and it costs the entire society. A large number of kids these days are looked after by their grandparents. I have explained earlier the pros and cons of this. The outcome of this high divorce rate is that kids are not properly housed, fed, or clothed because the supporting parent does not have enough income to run the house. Many grandparents are not wealthy enough to run two households. Running a wholesome household requires two incomes. Child support and alimony are sought by the parent with kids from the other spouse but most of the time, they do not pay—and even if they do pay, the amount stipulated is usually not enough. Many kids are not adequately supervised or disciplined and are usually left to fend for their own while the parent is at work. This causes poor attitudes, lack of proper supervision, and poor grades in school. The entire community suffers from poorly raised children who grow up with a higher tendency to run afoul of the law.

Overly Litigious Society

America has slowly become a lawsuit-happy society. As the population gets more educated and sophisticated and has more knowledge about the laws and the legal system, more people are suing for frivolous, petty things. Neighbors sue one another about broken fences, relatives sue one another about a small loan given for some urgent necessity, consumers sue the businesses for such things as finding a pit in a salad that caused a toothache or spilling a hot coffee, and the list goes on. Celebrities, athletes, and other wealthy people file for divorces and their ex-spouses sue for millions of dollars to maintain their luxurious lifestyles. All this sets bad examples to the rest of the public.

This type of frivolous and vexatious lawsuits gives a bad reputation to the legal system and waste of time of the court system. At times, insurance companies have to step in and defend cases. Insurance premiums go up. To protect himself, a prudent citizen has to purchase all types of insurance—auto, employment liability, homeowners, and often an umbrella policy and many different types of liability policies. Unnecessary litigation raises the costs of health care, goods, and services. It clogs the court system. It creates distrust and anger amongst friends and family members. It has gone so bad that some courts have a policy that one cannot file more than a certain number of cases in one year, especially in small-claims courts.

People are scared that if they take one wrong step they will get sued. The presence of a huge number of attorneys who are willing to take on these unmeritorious cases compounds the problems. In the 1980s, America had two-thirds of all the attorneys in the world and they were all doing well. They were often seen as part of the problem for filing outlandish lawsuits—and often it was done to harass and frustrate the defendants. Some of them were called ambulance chasers while others were called hungry attorneys trying to make a living by taking on scum-of-the-pond cases.

For some people, this is an easy way to win some money and share it with their attorneys. Many lazy people who are not willing to work hard and make their money honestly will look for opportunities to sue someone.

Be careful and watch your actions and words while dealing with strangers—as well as your acquaintances. Some people will file a lawsuit if you criticize them in public—even though the criticism had merit and comes under freedom of speech privileges. The other lesson is to cover yourself with good insurance policies. Having good insurance coverage is very important in this country, especially if you own a house or other expensive assets. If you run a business, then workers' compensation insurance is mandatory. A general liability insurance policy will cover most of the cases where you are being sued for some type of property damage or for negligently causing personal injuries.

Lack of Leisure Time

I have worked in this country continuously for more than thirty years and have the experience and some basic knowledge about basic labor laws and regulations. Since American workers are dedicated and hardworking, I strongly feel that American workers should be entitled to more paid vacations. We all like making money, want to have good jobs and careers, and want to become wealthy, but we all want to spend more time with our family and explore our hobbies and other interests. In America, lots of people work for years before they are entitled to fifteen days of paid vacation time. Some companies do not even give ten days of paid vacation to their junior employees. This makes working life for an average person very stressful and boring. Their sense of enjoyment of life is dimmed and their pride is diminished because they think all they are doing is work, work and more work. Some people work for more than forty hours a week with no overtime pay because they fear if they complain to their employer, they will get fired. People are standing in line to take their jobs.

I am interested in travelling and seeing other cultures and different countries. I am interested in visiting different parts of the United States, but I do not get enough paid vacation time to do these interesting things. In other countries, such as Italy and France, they get close to forty days of paid vacation under the labor laws. With so many days off, they can balance their lives with leisure and work. Consequently, they have good family lives, better health, better knowledge about this world, and much happier lives.

American labor laws are somewhat harsh toward the workers and need to be revamped to give the workers more vacation time and better working conditions. Employers need to realize that their workers are their greatest asset and workers need to have time to relax. Some people wait until they are retired, but by then, their health may be too frail to travel or they may not have enough funds to enjoy traveling, golfing, boating, or other activities.

Traffic

Traffic congestion in this country is getting worse. My one-way commute to work is only about twenty miles, which according to American standards, is not too bad. It should only take forty minutes to get to my job, but it can take me ninety minutes if traffic is bad. If there is a bad accident, I can be delayed for a couple of hours. According to one survey, the average urban commuter is stuck in traffic forty-six hours a year. The traffic jams increase 30 percent faster than roads can be built in this country, showing that Americans are still in love with their automobiles and the nation's traffic problems are getting worse. Even in small cities, this problem exists and urban planners are lost and do not know what to do. Building roads and bridges is very expensive and cities need lots of federal and state fund assistance.

One statistic shows that in the eighty-five biggest cities, it costs travelers 3.5 billion hours of lost time per year. Los Angeles, San Francisco, Washington, Dallas, Atlanta, and Houston have the worst traffic jams.

America definitely needs more freeways, more roads, and better public transportation systems to alleviate this major problem. We need billions of federal dollars to make improvements in our highway systems. We need to get our commuters out of their vehicles and train them to travel by buses, trains, and ferries. Some of us are doing all of this, but it is not enough. Another alternative is user fees and toll roads. Under this system, motorists would be charged for driving in congested lanes during rush hours. Some states have implemented this system and are generating revenue to build more roads. Slightly higher taxes on gasoline will raise more money to build roads. One should not forget that the United States is one of the few places on this earth where gas and diesel prices are still relatively cheap and affordable.

No matter how bad the traffic problem gets in this country, America can still boast of having the best freeways, bridges, and interstate road systems in the world. The major freeways are safe, clean, nicely landscaped, and are fully protected by local police and patrol officers. Yet there is room for improvement. If people can get out of their cars and make use of the public transportation system, some of these traffic problems will be alleviated.

These are my pet peeves and if you ask my wife and my two daughters, they will have their own list of complaint about living in this great country. Our frustration and disappointments are always alleviated when we just think for a moment about our freedom, inalienable natural and human rights, democracy, civil liberty and constitutional government. I intently listen every day to some national politician who gives a speech about the decline of America and the fall of the greatest industrial republic in the world and how America is losing its superiority. There may be some element of truth in their assertions but the fact remains, America still retains the superpower status and it will take several decades for Europeans and Asians to catch up with America either economically or militarily. China is trying very hard to beat the American economy but there will be always that American ingenuity that will keep America a step ahead in the game. These are my observations and I sincerely hope that I will be proven right.

Chapter 18:
My Contributions to My Adopted Country

"The American middle class and low income workers striving to earn a middle class standard of living rely on the economic contributions of immigrants, both authorized and undocumented."

Drum Major Institute Report For Public Policy 2009

The debate about immigration has really heated up in the political arena over the past few years. Sometimes people get very passionate about this subject. After all, America is a nation of immigrants, so of course this is going to be a topic that is very close to the people's hearts. Americans welcome newcomers. Yet, part of the controversy of immigration policies has to do with the effect of new arrivals on our economy. Some argue that more people drain our resources and we should slow down the rate of new arrivals—at least until economic conditions improve. But is this really true? There is a controversy brewing that foreign born professionals who come to the United States on temporary visa (such as H-1B's) are somehow "stealing jobs" from native born workers. Hence a stop should be made to issuing these visas.

However, one must not overlook the statistics that show myriad ways in which highly skilled immigrants fuel the United State's economic growth through their innovation and business acumen. It would be wrong to stop these best and brightest people from coming to the United States for we stand to lose a lot. They will easily be accepted by other western countries where they will be taking their talents, skills, knowhow and investment dollars.

According to the president's council of economic advisors, US-born natives gain an estimated $37 billion a year from immigrant's participation in the American economy, including four categories that immigrants contribute immensely to the US economy. The statistics relating to the immigrant's economic contributions are eye opening.

- Immigrants contribute as workers. The Drum report cites that one in every four doctors in the United States is foreign born as well as one in three computer software engineers and more than 42 per cent of medical scientists.
- Immigrants contribute as consumers. The Drum report also mentions that immigration is a significant contributor to the rapid growth of the Hispanic and Asian American consumer markets that together accounted for an estimated $1.46 trillion in buying power in 2008.
- Immigrants contribute as entrepreneurs. Immigrant owned businesses employ American workers and raise capital from abroad to invest in the United States economy. The Drum report mentions that one in ten self-employed business people in the United States is an immigrant.
- Immigrants contribute as taxpayers. According to a landmark study by National Research Council an average immigrant pays $1800 more in taxes

than what he receives in public benefits. Over their lifetime, the average immigrant and his immediate family contributes over $80,000 more in taxes than they receive in benefits.

Many readers will ask how I have contributed to the country that has given me so much over the past three decades. What have I done in return? That will be a very fair inquisition and a candid response is warranted. I believe that it is unethical—and to a certain degree immoral—to migrate to a new country and take advantage of its resources, services, and benefits without giving anything back. A good, honest, loyal citizen always thinks about ways that he can reciprocate for his country. President John F. Kennedy said, "Ask not what your country can do for you—ask what you can do for your country." His words linger in my mind all the time. The best way of serving your country is to be a good, loyal, upright, and decent citizen. Try not to violate any laws, harm anyone, or do any illegal or criminal activity. Stay away from gangs and desperados, refrain from using any illegal drugs and do not unnecessarily seek any public assistance. Obey the laws and always act as a thorough gentleman—that is the ideal way to live in any country. President Woodrow Wilson's said, "Democracy exists for the purpose of reducing inhumanity and maximizing hope." We have come to live in this country not only to enjoy its benefits, but also to contribute to its development in whatever way we can.

I am not going to deny the fact that I could have done more for my country than what I have contributed so far. I could have volunteered and contributed more. I could have sought public office or registered for the Army Reserve. Instead, I focused mainly on myself and raising my family. It was the right thing to do because charity begins at home. I am hoping that when I retire in a few years, I will be able to devote a lot of my time to doing charitable and social work in my community. Thus, the intention, desire, and determination have not shifted- to help others as much as I can in any shape or form. As I reflect on my thirty years in this country, I think I have made some very positive contributions.

Education

I arrived in this country with a degree in law. I did all my schooling in Fiji and New Zealand and had a few years of experience in practicing British-style law. When I arrived in this country, I went straight to work. Since I was willing to take any type of employment, I had no problem in landing a paralegal position with a small law firm in Livermore. I did not have to go to school or have to get any legal training. I did not have to get any education loans or scholarships to get my first job. I was fortunate, the quality of my education was of such a high standard that when the senior partners of the firm interviewed me, they were confident that I could do the job. Deep inside, I knew that I would have to educate myself as I went along, but the very thought that I was imbued with great education made me confident that there was nothing impossible. I did not care if I had to work late and long hours. I did not care that I was being paid far less than other law firms were paying their paralegals. I did not have any concerns about new challenges in my new work environment. I was just happy that I had a job. Back then, the economy was doing poorly and the unemployment rate was high. I was delighted to have a job in the same field that I had been educated and trained in.

The United States immediately benefited from my education and did not have to spend a dime in educating or training me. I arrived in this country and started contributing to the economy immediately. I bought a car, rented an apartment, bought furniture, tools, household appliances, and clothing, and hooked up cable, electricity, and water. Everyone benefited immediately from my presence. My contributions were beneficial to my entire community. In addition, I paid my share of taxes.

One report shows that most immigrants arrive in the United States during their prime working years. More than 70 percent of immigrants are over eighteen when they arrive. The report states that there are roughly 17.5 million immigrants in the United States who were educated in their native countries. "The windfall to the US of obtaining this human capital at no expense to American taxpayer is roughly $1.43 trillion. This makes immigration a fiscal bargain for our country" is a commentary worthy to take note of.

Great Work Ethic

During one of my annual performance review, my manager said, "We can teach our employees everything about how to best do their job. We can train you folks. We can teach you. We can give you all the resources and tools—and we can send you for advanced training. But, we cannot teach an employee how to be punctual, how to be at work every day, we cannot teach them how to be pro-active, and we cannot teach them how to be loyal, trustworthy, reliable, and hardworking. We see a lot of these wonderful qualities that managers look for in foreign-born workers like you." Of course, he gave me a good raise and an outstanding evaluation. There may be some truth in this manager's observations.

Much research done by big corporations has revealed that foreign-born workers have better work ethics. Of course, there are many exceptions. There may be some cultural issues, upbringing, discipline issues, or bias—or it could be attributed to strict parenting. The point is that immigrants have a good track record for being exceptionally good workers—in blue-collar jobs and white-collar jobs.

Business Contributions

About fifteen years ago, my wife and I bought a pizza restaurant with the idea that we would operate and build it up so that we could do something when we retired. We were thinking of retiring early and thought that it would give us a wonderful opportunity to employ some young people and take advantage of owning a franchised restaurant business. Sadly, it was not a wonderful, lucrative experience since we lost some money and found it to be very labor-intensive business. Nevertheless, we operated and owned it for almost ten years.

During our ownership, we employed a number of local young people and paid them well. We sponsored a number of local baseball, soccer, and football teams and helped them out by buying uniforms and boots etc., We sponsored some bands and helped them out in displaying their talents in public. We even helped them pay for their recordings and promotions. We helped a number of homeless and disabled people who desperately needed food and clothing. In addition, we paid our fair amount of taxes to the federal, state, and city government, and other agencies, such as the Alcohol Beverage Agency, the environmental agency, and the county health department. On top of that, we had to pay franchise fees, advertising fees, and a bunch of other promotional expenses.

We were enmeshed with the local community and provided monetary and food assistance without a second thought. Everyone benefited—our business thrived, the community received assistance and overall, it created good vibes and a sense of contentment.

Community Service

Despite my hectic lifestyle and demanding work schedules, I have been able to expand and enrich my spiritual life. America has given me the inspiration, strength, encouragement, and freedom to cultivate my own religion, culture, and traditions. I am of East Indian origin and a devout Hindu. Over the years, I have studied and practiced my religion in a very sincere and faithful manner. My father has been a Hindu pundit for many years and has encouraged me to become a pundit too. He told me that I would get a lot of satisfaction in helping out our community by way of advice, performing marriages, funerals, and other important Hindu rituals and ceremonies. Hinduism is a very ritualistic religion and, unless certain rituals are done in the right manner, it does not give much credence to the significance of the ceremony.

Taking my father's advice to heart, I slowly learned Sanskrit mantras, sacred scriptures such as Vedas, Gita, and Puranas, how to do rituals at weddings and funerals, and have gradually become a pundit myself. I am invited to people's homes almost every weekend and promote my religion. At the same time, I perform special ceremonies and prayers for those who are desirous to practice their Hindu faith.

This sort of interaction with my community and helping out in some small way to promote Hindu religion gives me great satisfaction. The community receives the benefit of my religious knowledge. I get their blessings and good wishes in return. The entire society benefits from this humanitarian contribution. Praying with people, sharing their pains and pleasures, listening to their beliefs and ideologies, and talking to the sick and elderly brings happiness to so many faces—it enriches and refines their lives. There is nothing more joyful or rewarding than sharing aspects of your spirituality and knowledge with your friends, relatives, and acquaintances. The freedom of religion that this country allows its citizens to practice and promote is one of the greatest and most fundamental freedoms that any country can give to its people.

Paying Taxes

During my three decades in this country, I have paid more than three quarters of a million dollars in taxes to the state, federal and local governments. My wife and I have paid income taxes, business taxes, franchise taxes, sales taxes, unemployment taxes, vehicle taxes, property taxes, transfer taxes, municipal taxes, and transportation taxes. The list of different types of taxes imposed in this country is endless specially if you own a business. Every time I pay these taxes, I remind myself that this is what gives us good roads, infrastructure, public transportation, library, police and fire departments, and civic administrators. I have paid—and continue to pay—taxes in all aspects of my life. Whether I buy groceries, clothes, furniture, cars, or gasoline, taxes have to be paid. A fair taxation system is what keeps the American economy buoyant. I realize that we have to pay as we go, but the gripe that I have is that taxes are not equitably assessed. Some large corporations hide behind a corporate veil and all sorts of exemptions in order to avoid paying their share of taxes. Tax assessment in this country has to be done more equitably is another one of my gripes.

The fact that immigrants contribute their fair share of taxes is an understatement. They usually pay more than their fair share because they do not have many exemptions. One report estimates that new immigrants will provide four hundred and seven billion dollars to the Social Security system over the next fifty years. The Congressional Budget Office says, "Over the past two decades, most efforts to estimate the fiscal impact of immigration in the United States have concluded that in aggregate and over a long term, tax revenues of all types generated by immigrants—both legal an unauthorized—exceed the costs of the services they use."

In view of the above, you can argue on very solid grounds that immigrants are not a burden to this society; to the contrary, they are a boon. Immigrants make great contributions in the form of taxes that benefit the American economy.

Responsible and Caring Citizens

Every country wants responsible, patriotic, law-abiding citizens. They want hardworking people that are able to pay their own way until they become physically disabled or retire. There is usually no appreciation for people who are lazy, have vices such as drug and alcohol addiction, have no objective in life, and become a burden to the society. Fortunately, I have been lucky. I have managed to be a law-abiding citizen, have never taken any welfare benefits, and have never tried to lie, deceive, or cheat any of the systems to obtain any assistance. Being a model citizen is what I perceive as my great contribution to our country. My wife and I have given thousands of dollars to numerous charities and have helped out with clothing, furniture, and schoolbooks at my daughter's special children's school. We give money to food banks, the Special Olympics, and the Special Children's Fund. We find it hard to say no to administrators of local charities. The idea of helping and assisting the less fortunate is ingrained in my habits. The day I stop helping less fortunate human beings will be the darkest day of my life. Millions of immigrants who arrive in this country from Third World countries have the same type of mentality—and charity is of paramount importance to them. They have been taught to help others since their childhood and they are eager to help and assist whenever and however they can.

I am just one immigrant who has tried to do what is right, civil, and humanitarian for the promotion and strengthening of my adopted country. I am anxious to find other means and ways to contribute to my country—my money, knowledge, skills, or talents—no matter in what manner I can contribute, I am determined to help my country. Millions like me try to do the proper thing on a daily basis. I realize that there are—and will be—some who will not be able to contribute too much to society due to health, family, work, or financial reasons. We need to pray for these the unfortunate people, but the majority of us are healthy, capable, have a few extra dollars, and can give something back to our country. It does not matter what form that contribution is going to be as long as there are good intentions. If all American-born citizens and immigrants are motivated to contribute something to this wonderful country in some small way, then America —and not India or China—will be the greatest country of this century once more. The citizens of a country is its greatest and most precious asset. And, it is incumbent on these citizens to do whatever it takes to make their country a better place to live. We just cannot depend on our government to provide everything for our livelihood and luxury living.

Chapter 19:
Things I Miss Most About Fiji

Having been born in the beautiful Fiji Islands, I was fortunate enough to spend the first eighteen years of my life in Fiji. I have come a long way from when I was a boy growing up in Fiji, but so much of my ancestral homeland remains inside of me—and I believe that it will forever. This is the place where I find my roots, including my earliest memories. I received my primary education in the public schools, which were of average standard. I learned a lot from the hardworking, dedicated teachers. The secondary school education was also of average standard. The school buildings and facilities were decrepit, but the teachers rallied around their students to make them successful in studying for and taking the overseas exams. I managed to pass the New Zealand certificate and proceeded to get further education in New Zealand before entering into university in Auckland. I have deep gratitude and appreciation for my motherland. I was born there, spent my childhood there, and will never forget spending my youth in such a beautiful, peaceful country. My deep appreciation and gratitude also extends to the wonderful teachers at Tilak High School in Lautoka, Fiji, and at D. A. V. College in Suva, Fiji.

When I reminiscence, there are certain things that I miss, but I remind myself that I had a choice. I could have stayed and raised my children in the island country and would have fully enjoyed my legal career. However, I chose to emigrate to America and thus, the first chapter of my life ended when that choice was made. I must confess that, during my first two years in America, I got the inclination on a number of occasions to return to Fiji to reestablish my life there. I could have easily replanted myself from where I had uprooted myself. The expense and hassle would have been minimal and it would have required very little time, effort, or energy because I knew the socioeconomic system and the people.

However, I kept on getting cold feet and could not gather enough courage to tell everyone that I was going back. I always thought that only losers went back to the place that they have left voluntarily. I could not make myself turn around and go back. In addition, I had the drive and desire to succeed in the United States. I reminded myself that others had done it and I could too.

It reminded me of a true story of an English immigrant family who were on the dock in Liverpool, England. This man, his wife and two children were getting ready to board the ship to emigrate to America. Just before the ship was to sail, the husband suffered a momentary panic and announced that he was going to retrieve his baggage from the hold of the ship and return to his leased farm. His wife quickly reminded him that he had no home to return to since they had sold everything. He eventually and reluctantly got on the ship. The voyage lasted two and half months. After their arrival in Illinois and experiencing the bitter cold winter, they all deeply regretted having left England. But after fifteen years of unremitting toil, they became owners of three hundred acres of farmland, a big house and abundance of livestock, farming implements and so forth. In one of his letter to their relatives the husband wrote that in their new country, there was no lack of good food, such as beef, pork , butter, fowls, eggs, milk, flour, fruits and happiness abounded. They were thrilled to bits that they decided to migrate. Instead of being struggling tenant farmers who were just getting by in England, their hard work and opportunities in America had made them wealthy and prosperous land-owners. The lesson here is that the husband's moment of panic on the dock at Liverpool had not aborted his dream of success in America.

I had the same type of anxiety and confusion in my mind that haunted me from time to time. Slowly but surely, it all vanished. In spite of everything that I quickly amassed and acquired in America, I still miss certain things about Fiji that cross my mind every now and then. These treasured memories remind me how fortunate I was to spend some magical years of my life in the wonderful country of my birth.

Some things that I missed immensely about Fiji when I first arrived in this country were:

Familiar Surroundings and Friends

I missed my friends and some dear family members that we left behind. We lived in a small town and had known a lot of people— some became good friends, visiting and socializing with us on a regular basis. These caring, generous, and loving people were part of our social circle. We left them behind. They felt betrayed and I was filled with a sense of being selfish. In America, we had to start all over again with a totally different socializing process. Since this was a much bigger society comprised of different races, cultures, traditions, and values—and everyone minded their own business—making friends was initially very difficult.

In the old country, we knew by heart the neighborhood streets, shops, and restaurants. We even knew our friends' vehicle license plate numbers. We knew who lived on which street without checking the address book. We used to drive around familiar places where we first met our girlfriends, where we played in our first soccer matches, or where we first drank liquor outside our home. We remembered with great accuracy our rented homes, our schools, and birthplaces—even the location of our tailor, barber, and butcher—and a number of other memorable things. Familiarity breeds security, reliability, and confidence. All that familiarity about our surroundings and environment vanished once we got on the airplane and departed for America.

Small Society

The beauty of living in a small society was also beneficial since we knew our neighbors, our local police officers, and our religious and political leaders quite well. Knowing prominent people—sometimes on a first-name basis—and their family members gave us a sense of importance and prominence. We knew we could get any type of problem resolved by making few phone calls or contacting friends who held important positions in government or private sectors.

Living in a small close-knit society taught us how to respect and treat people with dignity and sensitivity. The elders were given priority status and respect. Growing old in the old country was not too much of a problem for our elders because their children always were expected to look after them. Living in a close-knit society made wonderful things such as love, bonding, courtesy, respect, appreciation, and gratitude second nature for us.

Carefree Lifestyle

The carefree lifestyle that one becomes accustomed to—and which becomes a norm after a while—was one thing that I initially missed a lot. No matter where one went—government offices, lawyer's office, doctor's office, or police station—the social atmosphere was always very casual and relaxed. Everyone took their time in doing the paperwork and talked about our lives before getting down to business. Some places had yongona (kava) readily made and the attendant would offer you a bowl of yongona before starting the business. Everything was done in a casual manner with a lot of time allowed for non-business socialization. Everyone dressed casually—even at weddings and important parties. Nothing got started on time because no one made any effort to arrive on time. Private functions always got started late since the guests invariably arrived late, but no one complained. The only place that there was some respect for time was in the court system where the judges and magistrates always started the proceedings on time. Latecomers were usually reprimanded. During the weekends, when we went out shopping or to the local market, almost half a day would go by meeting friends and chatting. A few hours would easily elapse before we would start buying our vegetables or groceries. In a small place, everyone knows one another and markets, stores, and public streets are good socializing venues. There was no sense of urgency or desire to rush in doing anything. Life was simply too simple and carefree; nothing was more important than having a good time with friends and families. The kids were allowed to play outside in the open. There was no fear by the parents about kidnapping or molestation. The parks, backyards, and streets were always abuzz with the shouting and yelling of happy kids.

Since most of the mothers did not go out to work, the kids had lots of time to bond with family and they received proper care and love. The idea of finding a babysitter was largely unheard of. Every family had friends, relatives, or grandparents ready and willing to look after young children. When children went home from school, mothers or grandparents welcomed them. The vision of latchkey children was just that—a vision. This in turn promoted healthy families and good bonding.

Recreational and Leisure Time

The British, who governed Fiji for more than one hundred years, set aside lots of public holidays based on the British system. Holidays were celebrated for the queen's birthday, Prince Charles' holiday, Bank holiday, and Easter holidays—the list was pretty long with close to two dozen public holidays. We had a lot of spare time away from work or school for ourselves and for families. It enabled us to foster our own hobbies and passions, such as fishing, boating, picnicking, playing soccer or rugby, or repairing our cars or houses. There was plenty of time to do things that we would not otherwise have time to do. Going to movies, cultural shows, or the beach were popular pastimes.

Natural Beauty

The islands have a natural romantic and enchanting beauty. Turquoise-blue seawater, white sandy beaches, coconut trees, and mangroves added splendor and beauty to the shoreline. One could spend many hours hiking into the mountains or riverbanks or spending leisure time eating sugar cane, coconuts, guavas, mangoes, or pineapples taken fresh from the fields.

Fiji—with three-quarters-of-a-million people—had less traffic, crowded streets, pollution, traffic noise, hustle and bustle, traffic lights, and congestion than my new country did. Since everyone had big backyards (about a quarter-acre), there was plentiful space to plant cash crops and vegetables. Many people even raised chickens, ducks, or goats. Beautiful sunrises and sunsets, clear skies, tropical warm rains, refreshing sea breezes, and the lush landscape with little commercial development made the islands of the South Pacific a paradise to live in.

Cheap Living

Since the standard of living was not high back then and the hourly wage rates were low, we found that groceries, meat, and vegetables were quite cheap and affordable. I made a good living wage. Hence, the cost of living was evidently cheap for me. The fresh vegetables and fruits could not be beat. Housing was very affordable and many rental units were always on the market with open porches and backyards. No one lived on the streets or slept in the parks. Everyone was taken care of by their family—whether they had any money or not. It did not matter if a family member had no job or income. It did not matter if they had some vices and abuse problems. At the end of the day, everyone had a home and food.

Proximity

The small size of the country made everything within reach. The airports, seaports, offices, grocery stores, and shopping plazas were located within fifteen minutes from home. Unlike in my chosen country—where it takes sometimes up to an hour to travel twenty miles—everything was located close to home and we spent little time in traffic. Schools, hospitals, and offices were only a few minutes away by car and maybe longer by a bus. If anyone put seven thousand miles on his car in a year, it would amount to above-average driving and the owner would be blamed for running around unnecessarily. There was a sense of security in knowing that everything was within an arm's length if something was needed.

Less Crime and Drugs and No Gangs

One of the first things that a person wants to know before moving into any neighborhood is the frequency of crime in the area. They need to know if it is infested with drug dealers, pimps, and gangs. In Fiji, property crime was very low because everyone's property rights and ownership were respected. The courts imposed tough sentences on intruders. The violence rate was very low in the entire country. If there were six homicides in the entire country, then it was too much and the religious leaders and politicians would demand answers from the police commissioner.

Gang activities were unheard of. If and when gang actions were spotted, local police and community leaders would quickly put an end to it. There was no fear of becoming a victim of gangs.

It was a very safe society—and completely safe to walk the streets at night. Some streets did not have streetlights in big towns because the crime rate was so low. Shops and restaurants did not have any window shutters and the banks did not have any security guards at the front door. It was a very safe and secure place. The villagers were even safer since everyone knew one another. Everyone left windows open at night to let in the fresh air.

Good Weather

Living in a tropical country has its advantages and disadvantages, but the advantages far outweigh the adversity. Throughout the year, the seasons remained almost the same with little variation in temperature. Hot weather throughout the year meant fewer blankets, less clothing, less insulation in houses, and less use of electricity. It boiled down to cheaper utilities. Lots of homes did not even have a washer or dryer since hand-washed clothes could easily be dried outside. The smell of clothes drying in the open sun lingers in my nose. Air-conditioning and coolers were luxuries. Warm weather meant more outside sports activities, an open-air lifestyle, and more opportunities to spend time at beaches, rivers, and pools. The rainy season brought plenty of rain, but sometimes hurricanes and floods wreaked havoc. Residents have learned to live with these natural calamities. Early warnings of flooding and hurricanes from meteorological offices reduced death and destruction to bare minimal.

Great People in a Multiracial Society

Fiji is known for people of different races living in peace and harmony. The indigenous Fijians and Indians, Chinese, Caucasians, and other Pacific Islanders live in harmony. Even during the days when I was in Fiji, friendly, generous smiling people were its greatest asset. The tourism industry was built around having very friendly people working in hotels, restaurants, immigration, customs, and government departments. One only had to stop by at anyone's home during lunchtime or dinnertime and you would not be allowed to leave without having some food and drinks. If you had car problems anywhere at any time, strangers would step out of their homes to help fix the car or get you other type of help. At weddings and other big functions, scores of people would show up voluntarily to assist the hosts with cooking, decorations, money, and clothes.

Since my departure, Fiji has unfortunately undergone some drastic changes. When we think about changes—it is usually for the better. Fiji, sadly, has gone through changes that have had adverse effects on its citizens, its economic progress, and its political process. The tiny island nation has dealt with four military coups backed by military leaders, and economic recession of unfathomable degree caused by the worldwide economic downturn. The political sea change caused by military coups has affected and touched the young and old, the rich and poor, and the farmers, business owners, and ordinary folks in tiny villages.

The coups are the worst thing that could ever happen to any developing nation. The coups have made Fiji a less desirable place to live. The unstable government, inept civil servants, rampant corruption, and unethical politicians have driven many thousands of its citizens out of the country. During the past twenty-five years, several thousand have left for affluent countries, such as Australia, New Zealand, Canada, and the United States. Some have left because of personal safety concerns; some have left because they feared their personal property and possessions being confiscated by unscrupulous leaders, much like what Idi Amin did to his wealthy citizens of Indian descent in Uganda many years ago.

The constant bickering, nasty political in-fighting, and hostile attitude of two major political parties—the Alliance Party and the Federation Party—have left a bitter taste in the mouths of Fiji's citizens. The young became restless; the older ones felt very scared; the educated felt vulnerable—and they all left the country in droves seeking better life in a foreign land. The loss of best and brightest doctors, entrepreneurs, business owners, teachers and hardworking cane farmers has had a daunting effect on the country's economy. The racial harmony has gone sour. The Indians and the native Fijians have not been able to amicably resolve the ownership of land issues which is a major bone of contention between the two races.

The military backed successive governments and their leaders have failed miserably to keep the sugar and tourism industries buoyant and lucrative. These two industries have been the backbone of Fiji's economy for a long time. Because of inefficiency and the poor and superficial policies of the government, the country has in many ways gone backward. Numerous factories have closed; many five-star hotels and resorts have had to deal with 50 percent reductions in business for many years. Farmers abandoned their fertile sugar cane farmlands, which then reverted into jungles. Businesses left the country because of the unstable government. Thousands were left jobless. All these negative things that have occurred during the past twenty-five years have made Fiji a much poorer country—not only economically, but also the entire grassroots fabric of the society has been left demoralized.

It is my cherished wish, hope, and prayer that one day in the not-too-distant a future, my country of birth will bounce back and regain its lost luster. It can become a gorgeous, thriving, and peaceful country once again. It definitely will have to start with the establishment of a solid democratic government.

I remember many years ago when I was vacationing in Fiji, someone asked me "what do you miss about Fiji ?" My instant answer was "everything " The next question was "so why live in the United States ?" My answer was " I wanted to live the American Dream ". I know it did not make any sense to the interviewer because of my double talk but it showed that I was still not quite sure about my motives to migrate. It also showed that a part of me was still languishing in the laps of my motherland.

As time went by and I became more engrossed in adjusting to my life in America, the things that I initially missed have become cherished memories. It is good to have wonderful memories stored in the back of your mind. It gives you good insight as to how other people live in different parts of the world. It also makes you realize that having plenty of money and being surrounded by material things does not give a person contentment and happiness. You have to live with the ideal philosophy that simple and ordinary things in life can bring joy and happiness. Happiness sometimes means overlooking the imperfections and accepting what we have and what we have achieved with hard work, sweat, toil, and tears.

CHAPTER 20:
WHY IMMIGRANTS REMAIN ATTACHED TO THEIR MOTHERLAND

My American friends and colleagues often ask why immigrants stay so attached to their native countries. Some are curious to know why we keep sending remittance to our distant cousins or why we keep on talking with them over the phone and e-mailing on regular basis. Some ask why we send clothes, bedding, and shoes when we should be looking after our own welfare first. These are fair questions and need to be explained.

Maybe it is impossible for somebody who has never moved away from the country of his or her birth to fully understand or appreciate an immigrant's story. Pulling up your roots, crossing the ocean, and adopting a new country can be a traumatic experience. Even though we may love our new adopted country, there will always be a certain calling somewhere deep within our hearts and minds that sings to us of the place that we originally called home. A motherland can be defined as a country that a person views as his or her country of origin or it could be the home of the person's ancestors. The extent of attachment varies considerably from person to person. One researcher found that about 10 percent of immigrants can be considered highly attached to their home country, but about 63 percent show moderate attachments to their motherland. A large majority of immigrants keeps some type of contact with their motherland. The older they were when they migrated to America, the more connection they have with their motherland. Some of them still have their parents and siblings living in the old country because not everyone has the opportunity to emigrate. The younger American-born generation usually does not know much about their parents' land of birth and they really do not care. However, there are children who do take a keen interest in their parents' motherland and are ready and willing to visit the old country to learn more about their roots. Getting to know about your roots is strongly emphasized by older immigrants. Children, as they grow, seem to show more and more interest in exploring their ancestors' history and background.

What are the reasons for being so strongly attached to one's motherland? The answer can be found in many forms. It could be that some have a more favorable view of their old country. Some have loved ones still living back at home, especially elderly parents and siblings. Some are not quite ready emotionally to let go of their profound feelings about their motherland. Clinging to the motherland can be a way to cope with culture shock for some people. It gives them something to hold onto as they struggle to adjust to a new place and culture. Whatever the reasons, it is in many ways advantageous to keep some sort of connection with your old country rather than cutting loose the ties.

As I think about my own family, most of them have been in America for more than three decades. Most are well to do in their own right. Most left their motherland with some hesitation because they knew there was no place like home. Nevertheless they emigrated, got settled in America, and have prospered. Some have made great progress in their standard of living, but a good number are still struggling with the American way of life. Some have no relatives or friends back in the motherland because many have migrated to different countries, some family members have died, and some have just moved on, cutting all ties with people living abroad. In spite of all this, I have noticed that the majority of my family still dearly loves their motherland. They regularly read news about Fiji on the Internet, listen to Radio Fiji, go there for vacation, and help out with donations and other necessities in times of crisis and natural catastrophes. The deep-rooted sentimental feelings for their motherland will never cease—no matter how many years they spend in America.

My personal reasons for keeping some contact with my motherland are few, but very genuine.

The Soil on Which One Is Born Should Never Be Forgotten

A Russian proverb says, "A person without a motherland is like a nightingale without a song." Most religions reinforce the idea that we should never forget the country in which we were born and raised. One is indebted to his motherland eternally. Even Rig Veda—the most revered scripture of Hindus, written about 4,000 years ago—says, "One should respect his motherland, his culture and his mother tongue because they are givers of happiness." Your native country gave you and your ancestors its air to breathe, its land to cultivate and to plant food, its natural resources to enjoy, its government to protect and serve you, its public facilities to be used, and its passport to travel all over the world. Your motherland is the place where once upon a time all of your relatives and friends lived. Your motherland is the place where many of your dead relatives and friends are buried. Abandoning one's motherland would not be moral or ethical by any stretch of the imagination. No wonder immigrants sometimes say that their cherished wish is to return to their motherland just before their death and, if possible, to die there.

During the recent World Cup soccer tournament, I noticed that my fellow immigrants wanted their boys from back home to win. They would stay home from work to watch the games being played by their home team, cheering for their boys and praying for a win. Even when the United States played, a lot of them cheered for their homeland, knowing full well they would be called traitors. But, they were willing to take the risk. All this boils down to the point that you can never shake off your strong feelings for your motherland—no matter where in the world you reside.

Guilt, Betrayal, and Selfishness

A large percentage of us, especially those who attained a high level of education in our home country, feel guilty that we left our country in our prime when we could have contributed a lot. When I was leaving Fiji, many of my friends were also migrating to different countries. The politicians and media people during those days were writing about brain drain and I could not quite understand what they meant. I thought there would be others who would step in my shoes and continue with good work for their country. I assumed that other highly qualified and motivated people would play our roles. When I arrived in America, I realized that my community was poorer for having lost me. It was heart wrenching to see the finest doctors, engineers, and tradesmen leaving their country of birth and migrating to industrialized countries all over the world.

Feelings of betrayal, unfaithfulness, and disloyalty linger in your mind. There may be a shadow of truth in them. We feel strongly that, by keeping some type of connection with our motherland, we can receive some consolation in the fact that at least we have not severed our ties completely.

Always Ready and Willing To Help

This is another reason for keeping in contact with our motherland. It is a well-known fact that the majority of immigrants sends money back home and regularly calls relatives and friends. Besides sending money, immigrants send all sorts of other stuff to friends and relatives back home as gestures of goodwill and out of a sense of charity. We keep a close watch and always ask whether the children need money for education, money is needed when someone gets sick and cannot work, the elderly have enough medicine, or if the house needs any urgent repairs. If we get any indication that help is needed, we readily respond. Usually it does not matter if we have financial problems and limitations in America. The opportunity to help the less fortunate is a mantra taught by all religions and practicing it gives a sense of charity, bliss, and serenity.

A Great Place to Vacation

We love vacationing in our country of birth. In fact, this is one of the reasons why some immigrants do not want to surrender their homeland's passport and are not interested in becoming naturalized American citizens. Since we are already familiar with the local restaurants, hotels, beaches, shopping malls, and major tourist resorts, we feel at ease by going to our motherland. In addition, we tell ourselves that it would help the local economy if we spent some of our money there. We get to socialize with old friends and relatives and listen to their tales about life in the old country. Some tales are unpleasant, but most are about joy and happiness. Sharing, caring, and rejoicing are part of human nature. It is similar to going on a pilgrimage when we return into the arms of our motherland.

We often stay with relatives and friends because they insist. If we do not oblige, then they are offended. If we refuse, they will think that America has changed us. Lots money and weird ideas about relationships with relatives and friends have somehow messed up our thinking about family and relationships. They also will insist in providing transportation, food, and advice as to where to go and places to avoid.

When we visit our homeland, it gives us an opportunity to assess the socioeconomic condition of the country. We get a good idea of how our folks are doing and what they need to uplift their standard of living. It makes the trip more exciting than visiting some new, remote, and strange place with expenses that have to be paid through our noses. I have found that the folks still living at home have a lot of respect and regard for the visitors coming from abroad. They do not look at us as foreigners. This could be due to religious reasons where we are taught that any person who visits you is a God-sent guest and must be given the very best welcome. The very first time you meet them, you can see genuine love and affection brimming on their faces. Most of them simply have no ulterior motives. They are just thrilled to see you. Since most of us still speak our mother tongue, eat the same kind of food, have the same attitude, habits, and demeanor about things (only with slight modifications), we are not seen as foreigners. We are readily accepted as one of them. That is when we feel that although we may have changed a bit by American culture and habits, the folks at home have not changed. They are ready and willing to accept us into their folds once again.

Nostalgia for the Homeland

A high number of immigrants still believe that there is no place like home. It does not matter how luxurious a life we may have or how much wealth we may have amassed in America, immigrants always have a soft spot in their hearts for their motherland. Most immigrants, usually during the first couple of years, miss their friends, customs, and traditions. The lifestyle, weather, familiar environments, traditions, and culture always have a nostalgic effect. This is one of the reasons why some new immigrants only have to find any lame excuse to travel to their homeland for things such as weddings, family parties, or other celebrations—provided they can afford to do so. You can take a person out of a country, but you cannot take the country out of that person. Certain unforgettable things about your motherland are ingrained in your mind and hearts. Good and bad memories about experiences in your motherland will stay entrenched in your mind because that is where you were born and raised and worked. My teenage years in Fiji were probably the best years of my life. Those wonderful years can never be forgotten—no matter where I live. I still go and visit my old house, school, soccer field, and cinema every time I go to Fiji.

I will not sever my ties with my motherland. I will always be indebted to—and remember—my motherland with deep gratitude and sincere appreciation. It gave me a lot. It cradled, nourished, and raised me. It educated me and it made me brave and smart enough to go out in the world and face the realties in life. Readers may deduce that I have one foot in both countries—and there may be an iota of truth in that. Of course, I have an affinity for my motherland. However, it has to be made very clear that my bond with Fiji does not come at the expense of my love, loyalty, and commitment to the United States of America. There is a vast difference between ancestral pride and loyalty to your adopted country. Your ancestral country is your cradle and your country of choice is your golden saddle to ride into the sunset. As an American citizen, it is my paramount duty and moral obligation to give all that I can—in any shape or form—to my beloved America. It is where I live by choice and it is where I have comfortably spent my adulthood. It has made me what I am today. Without a doubt, it is where I will be exhaling my last breath.

My undying love for my motherland will keep on dancing in my heart, mind, and soul—and no weapon, power, or amount of wealth or luxury life will be able to change that. Love and pride for one's motherland is only natural—and nature cannot be ignored.

A world renowned poet Kipling, once wrote about his land of birth in these poetic words:

> *Our hearts are where they rocked our cradle,*
> *Our love where we spent our toil, and our faith, our hope,*
> *our honor,*
> *We pledge to our native, God gave all men all earth to love,*
> *But since our hearts are small, Ordained for each one spot*
> *should prove*
> *Beloved over all.*
>
> —Rudyard Kipling

CONCLUSION

"That is the true genius of America, a faith in the simple dreams of its people, the insistence of small miracles. That we can say what we think, write what we think, without hearing a sudden knock on the door. That we can have an idea and start our own business without paying a bribe or hiring somebody's son. That we can participate in the political process without fear of retribution and that our votes will be counted or at least in most of the time."

—Barack Obama, 2004 Democratic Convention

Almost one hundred and fifty years ago, my great-grandparents went from India to Fiji seeking new adventure and challenges in a new country, seeking a new place where they could freely, peacefully, and happily raise their family. They went there with dreams and aspirations for a much better life than what they had in India. They were anxious and desirous to raise their standard of living. However, their plight was different. They were indentured by the British colonial administrators and were actually taken to Fiji some twelve thousand miles away. They were lied to by the British; they were deceived and defrauded by the British who told them that life would be just great on an island nation not too far away from India.

Our ancestors thought, because of their ignorance, that they were going to a country where jobs were plentiful, wealth was abundant, and life was going to be easy after the indenture of five years had expired. So, they set sail in wooden sailing ships. Some of these ships were lost in storms. Some ran aground on the reefs and some passengers died on the ship from serious illnesses.

Once they arrived in the British crown colony of Fiji, they found the living conditions to be deplorable. It was completely the opposite to what they had been promised. Life was like living on a marooned island—most of it was just jungle with primitive living quarters, no water, electricity, or sewer. All they could see were acres and acres of sugar cane farms. Beyond that were just wild jungles. Making their home in the wilderness was extremely difficult. They went there as laborers to work on sugar cane plantations. They were bonded and they were fully controlled by British administrators. They did not have any freedom at all—no freedom of speech, no basic human rights such as where they can live, what type of work they could do, where they could send their children to school—nothing. It was all closely and strictly controlled by the British administrators. They were told where to live, where to work and for how long, how many hours. They were actually told not to protest, demonstrate, or complain about anything—otherwise they would be severely reprimanded, whipped, or exiled to the outer islands. The physical and mental abuse on their laborers inflicted by the British escalated to such level that it became intolerable. There was a major hue and cry both in India as well as in England and eventually the indenture system for the British crown colony of Fiji had to be stopped in 1920 . The only concession was that if any of the laborers chose to stay back on the island, they were given the permission to do so.

Despite all these nasty things that happened to them, they worked hard and toiled with their blood and sweat on their leased farms. They argued, protested for their basic human rights with the British in an amicable manner, and were able to remain in Fiji after their contract had expired. Then they worked on their own—farms, ranches, factories, offices, restaurants, and stores. They gradually made the island nation a paradise in the Pacific. They became owners of businesses, bought farms, started manufacturing small items, their sons and daughters went into law, medicine, accounting, engineering, architecture, politics, teaching and other professions. They became carpenters, plumbers, mechanics, and barbers. Through sheer hard work and sacrifices, indentured Indians made their adopted country of Fiji one of the most advanced island nations in the Pacific in less than one century.

About one hundred and twenty years later, as a third generation Fiji-Indian, I had the same mindset when I decided to migrate to the United States. I thought about my future, about the future of my children, and about my own wealth, disposition, and prosperity. My great-great-grandparents had the same mentality when they left their homeland. However, for me, things were a million times different and better—and a million times more exciting. I had choices: the choice to go to America, the choice to decide where I wanted to stay in America, the choice of what I wanted for a career, and the choice of how I was going to chart my destiny. I had all the freedoms when I arrived in this beautiful country: freedom of speech, freedom of religion, and freedom to travel. I was afforded all the opportunities to better my lifestyle within a very short time—as long as I had the ambition and determination to work hard. After all, we are masters of our own destiny. What a contrast between what my ancestors had to endure in their new country and the lifestyle which I began to enjoy immediately when I first arrived in this country.

Immigrants have different circumstances and motivations to migrate to a foreign country. Poverty, adventure, family unification, children's education, risk-calculation, and hopes, aspirations, and dreams to be better off, to live in freedom, escape oppression, and financially assist families back at home are the underlying common denominators. This was true for my great-great-grandparents one hundred and fifty years ago and it was true of me about thirty years ago. America is one of the very few countries that offer a person every opportunity to make rapid progress and prosper if one is determined to do so.

Personally, as I reflect and analyze my thoughts, I dare to say that I was also one of those who had come to the United States to chase the American dream. I feel deeply indebted to America for giving me that opportunity. I must confess that some of the things that I wanted to accomplish has still not come into my grasp. Whether I will be able to achieve all of that before I expire, remains to be seen.

The other thing that I am thankful for is that America showed me and gave me three great gifts as soon as I landed on its shores. America is the country where you can be assured of three basic human rights: security, equality, and liberty.

Security means protection from unfair and unreasonable actions by the government. Equality means that everyone is entitled to equal protection under the laws of the United States. Everyone is to be treated the same—regardless of their race, religion, or political beliefs. Liberty means fundamental freedoms, such as freedom to travel, freedom to carry arms, freedom of speech, and freedom of religion. All that an American citizen is required to do in this country is to obey the laws, pay taxes, attend school, and serve as a juror when called upon, and to vote in elections. There are four requirements for an individual to be eligible to vote a) be a citizen of America b) be a registered voter c) be over the age of eighteen and d) be a resident of a state . Most states require thirty days of residency.

Citizen responsibilities include being informed about the government, respecting the rights of others, and respecting diversity. Every citizen should be conscious of these grandiose rights and responsibilities at all times. If we came to this country to better our lives, then we are obliged to do things that would help our county. Things that I have mentioned as my contributions to this country should always be at the back of each immigrant's mind. You scratch my back and I will do the same for you. The moral is to never forget to give back to your adopted country in whatever way you deem fit.

Not everything in this country is great for everyone. Not everything is hunky-dory. Many have returned to their homeland out of frustration and disappointments. There are many who want to go back, but will not because they think that it will be seen by their countrymen as abject failure on their part. Many immigrants complain about racial discrimination, America's high crime rate and violence, bureaucratic local and state governments, expensive housing, and the difficulty of getting jobs. You always have to remember that real life isn't always going to be perfect or go your way. However, recurring acknowledgement of what is working in our lives has to be appreciated. Undoubtedly, things will go wrong from time to time, but you must not quit.

When things go wrong as they sometimes will,
When the road you are trudging seems all uphill,
When the funds are low and the debts are high and you want to
smile but you have to sigh,
When health is pressing you down a bit, rest if you must
but don't you quit,
Success is failure turned inside out, the silver tint on the
clouds of doubt
And, you can never tell how close you are; it may be near
when it seems afar,

So, stick to the fight when you are hardest hit,
It's when things go wrong that you must not quit.

—Anonymous

The fact remains and most will concur that an immigrant's standard of life is of much higher quality than what they had in their homeland. They have better schools to educate their children and they have top notch doctors and hospitals to take care of them if they become seriously ill. They can go to sleep at night in peace knowing that no police officer or desperadoes will break into their homes to interrogate or arrest them.

I, for one, like this country. It has given me everything that I had expected when I first landed on its shores. I arrived in this country with aura of great expectations and I must confess that most of those lofty expectations have been fulfilled. There are few hopes and aspirations that have been dashed but we cannot be too greedy. We have to be grateful and thankful for what we have. Any type of success is a journey not a destination. Success means many wonderful positive things for different people in different ways. For some, it may mean nice home, vacations, financial security, giving your children maximum security. For others, success means admiration by others, leadership etc., But, for most of us, success means freedom, self- respect, human rights and continually seeking more happiness and satisfaction from life. America is one country where every human being can achieve their targeted goal of being successful and prosperous during his or her lifetime. Of course, hard work, sacrifice, frugal lifestyle, little bit of luck, strong imagination, courage, determination, ambition to have a bright future and good graces are essential ingredients to become successful not only in America but in any country on this earth.

I had some very rough phases in my life in the United States especially during the first five years and had to struggle mighty hard, but those were growing pains. My brother Sunil Arvind Balram who sponsored me and did all of the paperwork for me for the American Embassy, had warned me that life will not be "bed of roses" when you first arrive in America. You will have to overcome many hurdles, obstacles and major difficulties while chasing your American dream. And, gosh! He was right. He deserves our sincere thanks. It also reminded me of a speech by President Abraham Lincoln wherein he stated "we can complain that rose bushes have thorns or we can rejoice that thorn bushes have roses". My wonderful parents also impressed upon me that if I wanted my life to be a bed of roses than it was up to me to cultivate that life with love, determination, ambition, hope and hard work. My heartfelt thanks and deep gratitude goes to them for being a rock of stability throughout my life, no matter what the circumstances.

Notwithstanding all of the trials and tribulations, today when I look in my rearview mirror, the big picture is success and prosperity. America has embraced me, taken care of my family; it has kept my family safe and secure. It has convinced me—beyond all reasonable doubts—that no matter where you live, nothing can compare to living in the great United States of America. I think I can speak for the majority that whether pushed here by persecution or pulled here by the lure of a better life, we immigrants are living our version of the American Dream. We are proud citizens of this great country and should always remember that America is the land of the free because it is the home of the brave people.

"I like to live in America, Okay for me in America!" I have sung this song from *West Side Story* a thousand times and it has become my mantra.

Om Shanti, Shanti, Shanti, Om

INDEX